BASICS

FACADE
APERTURES

\\ ROLAND KRIPPNER \\ FLORIAN MUSSO

BASICS

FACADE
APERTURES

BIRKHÄUSER
BASEL · BOSTON · BERLIN

TABLE OF CONTENTS

FOREWORD

The outer skin of a building fulfils a number of functions. It protects the interior from external influences – weather, temperature differences, or from being overlooked. It is not usually desirable to be sealed off hermetically, so that as well as offering protection, the facade must open up to the outside world, interact with it and admit air and light. Openings link the inside and the outside functionally and/or visually, and relate to the two to each other.

The present volume in the Basics series for students deals with designing facade openings in the general field of construction. The many demands made on a window are first explained clearly, and the structural detail needed to construct them is then discussed. The various components, structural types and materials are presented with their specific characteristics and tied into the context of the surrounding wall areas, with close attention paid to understanding how the transition from opening to wall should be achieved, and the way in which the different functions of a window are operated in strata. These observations relate to rooms lit from one side with apertures placed vertically in the wall. Here the focus is on windows; regardless of the size of the opening, similar demands are made on doors and fixed glazing, and the same principles applied.

The peripheral areas of a facade are important structurally, functionally and in terms of design, as well as the actual openings. Devices for controlling the light admitted, ventilation and heat insulation around the opening are also discussed.

Familiarity with the structures and components that can be used for designing windows and glazed doors is an important basis for design work by architects who wish to give facades an individual character and create a composition that is harmonious both inside and out.

Bert Bielefeld
Editor

INTRODUCTION

An opening or aperture is generally defined as an "open place, hole, gap". In a building, openings are defined as empty spaces left in the wall. If creating a protected space is the building's first priority, then the openings in the facades are the next, essential measure if the space is to be used.

Furthermore, openings are an essential architectural design element. Their dimensions and proportions, their position in relation to the water-bearing layer (waterproof skin) or to the surface concluding a space, their arrangement and relation to each other make a crucial difference to the design of buildings. The elements used to close the aperture are either movable, depending on their function (windows, doors; both are basic functional building blocks), or fixed (glazing).

Windows play a central part in planning openings. Their form (components, formats), arrangement and distribution over the facade are the building's visiting card. The division of the windows and the internal structuring of the glazed area is another important feature within the overall effect. Stylistic developments and craft skills are also clearly discernible in window forms.

Control devices are additional systems for apertures, beyond the doors and windows themselves. They make it possible to control permeability for light, air and heat precisely. The degree of comfort in the interior can be adapted to suit the level of demand and users' needs, according to the weather conditions.

A wide range of structural elements and systems are available. Familiarity with basic functional principles and general structural conditions makes it possible to develop effective strategies for planning openings in relation to a particular climatic situation. Here the design aspects interact closely with functional requirements and structural qualities.

Openings perform the same protective functions (against cold, damp, noise, fire and intruders) as the facade, but are thermal weak points in the building envelope, and require a new strategic approach given tightened energy requirements. Openings also create possibilities of access and define areas in the wall concluding the space that provide the room with light and ventilation, and makes it possible to look out from the inside.

Fig.1:
Opening in natural masonry

Fig.2:
Opening in solid timber wall (log construction)

Fig.3:
Round window (in a 1950s pavilion)

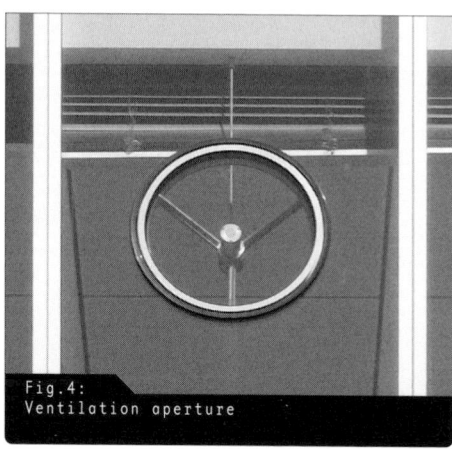

Fig.4:
Ventilation aperture

Fig.5:
Story-height openings

Fig.6:
Honeycomb openings

It therefore has to be possible to alter the permeability of these openings, so that the effects of heat, light and air can be regulated by special closing elements, appropriate to the location (changing climatic conditions) and the need for comfort (constant interior climate). The quality profile depends on position in relation to the sun, on considerations relating to the interior space, and on utilization.

Doors, which are older elements than windows in terms of architectural history, provide access to the building. They also include gates, although these are large and usually intended to be driven through. In most people's minds, openings in the facade more or less equate to windows. These are the elements that allow light to pass through transparent or translucent material even when they are closed, and allow air to flow in and out when the individual windows are open.

The simplest form of an element that closes apertures is fixed glazing. Lighting and ventilation can also be achieved separately from each other (e.g. a combination of window glazing and separately operated ventilation flaps).

Openings have a public aspect, facing outwards, which meets some of the demands made by prestige. Their number and size suggest the social status of owner and occupants. The inward-facing side has a character of privacy and intimacy. The arrangement of doors and windows influences the effect made by the interior as well. Rooms that are well provided with windows can seem more generous and airy than the real dimensions would convey.

PROTECTIVE FUNCTIONS

The basic needs that windows meet have remained largely the same for centuries, but there has been a considerable change in requirements for thermal and sound insulation and fireproofing, and for airtightness where the structural elements meet the wall. The demands made on a window's properties or efficiency depend on the location of the building – the topography, the direction in which it faces, and the height of the building, and are strongly affected by the prevailing wind.

Heat and sound insulation

The heat and sound insulation a window provides depend essentially on the material chosen for the frame and its structure or thickness, the nature and thickness of the glazing, and the way the component is fitted.

A window has to meet minimum heat insulation requirements and thus protect the interior against cold. As elements, frame and glass must be able to buffer temperature peaks between the interior and the exterior despite the relative thinness of the structural element. To avoid heat bridges the window should be positioned within the insulating layer of the wall as far as possible; and to avoid condensation and mold the interior surfaces should be at high temperatures. > Chapter Window components, Glazing systems

Spaces adjacent to the exterior wall should be insulated from the outside world in terms of sound. In most cases the interior should be protected from exterior noise (e.g. aircraft, road traffic, etc.), but the reverse is also true.

The required heat and sound insulation can be achieved by using special glass (heat and sound insulation glazing), or by the type of window

\\ Note:
In exterior walls and glazing in particular, the interior surface temperature affects the heat requirements and the sense of comfort. The temperature that users perceive is an average of air and surface temperature. Choice of material, wall structure and/or improved windows should be used to keep interior surface temperatures within the perceived temperature range.

\\ Note:
Accumulated condensation
If the water vapor in the (room) air cools to the extent that it becomes liquid, condensation forms. Surface temperatures should thus be kept as high as possible, especially for glazing and attachment points.

construction (winter, double-glazed, box-type windows). Improved heat insulation raises the surface temperatures for the glass pane on the interior side. This reduces the physiologically unpleasant presence of cold air in the window area. Better glass increases the demands made on the structural window components in terms of heating technology. Laminated, insulated timber frames or thermally separated metal elements improve the overall qualities of windows considerably.

Attention must be paid to protection against summer heat or overheating, as well as to winter heat insulation. This depends primarily on the size of the opening, as well as on the way the building faces.

Windows should not let in rain (and splash water) or dampness, as this would damage the fabric of the building.

To avoid drafts and ensure controlled ventilation the windows should have airtight fittings and fastenings. This applies above all to the joint with the building, but also to the one between the fixed frame and the opening section. Improved insulation standards diminish the impact of ventilation heat losses on the building's energy requirements.

Moisture from the interior affects the windows and their joints, along with the effects of the weather in general. In relation to water vapor diffusion, the principle applies that the functional layers should always be thicker inside than they are outside. This ensure perfect moisture transport through the building structure from the interior.

Large apertures need sight screening to ensure the privacy of the spaces behind them.

Glare is caused by marked light density contrasts, which are particularly disturbing in workplaces with monitors. Antiglare systems control

Your opinion is important to us

1. Please list the author and title of the book you purchased:

2. Please rate the book in the following areas:
1 = very good, 5 = poor

	1	2	3	4	5
Up-to-date					
Accurate					
Practical					
Language is clear and comprehensible					
Visual presentation (layout)					
Quality of illustrations/tables					
Organization, didactic approach					
Value for money					

3. How could the book be improved?

4. In which of the following areas do you have the greatest need for information?

- Design
- Technical Drawing
- Construction
- Profession
- Building Physics/Building Services
- Design Aesthetics
- Materials
- Landscape Architecture
- Town Planning
- Theory

5. What is a subject in which you feel a good textbook or reference work is still lacking?

6. Do you have any other comments? ...please send them to: feedback@birkhauser.ch

7. How did you find out about this book?

- Colleague
- Teacher
- Bookstore
- Publisher's catalogue
- Publisher's prospectus
- Journal
- Internet
- Review in
- Ad in
- Other

PRIORITY
PRIORITAIRE

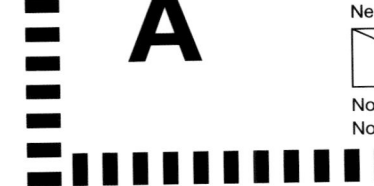

Ne pas affranchir

Non affrancare
No stamp required

Sender:

E-Mail:

I am
A student
A teacher

I would like to be kept informed of the publisher's
future publications.

Are you interested in becoming a Birkhäuser author?
If so, please contact the editorial department.

**RÉPONSE PAYÉE
SUISSE**

Birkhäuser
Viaduktstrasse 42
4051 Basel
Schweiz

www.birkhauser.ch

Fig.7:
Semitransparent antiglare system

Fig.8:
Protection against falling

> 💡

inward radiation, thus reducing the brightness differential between field of vision and computer screen.

Antiglare devices are place on the interior side. They should not completely block out daylight or make visual contact impossible. Systems that can be raised from the lower edge of the opening and positioned as wished without covering the whole surface of the glass are particularly suitable. > Fig. 7 Sight-screening can be placed outside, inside an additional-leaf window, or inside the room.

Fire protection Fire must not be allowed to break out in buildings, but if it does, the fire must not be allowed to spread. Fires can spread via apertures from room to room, and from story to story. Window frames and glazing are subject to fire protection requirements to limit fire spread. These have to be met by the frame materials and the glazing selected.

Impact resistance, fall protection In the case of story-high glazing in particular (shop windows, panoramic panes, etc.), window design can be affected by possible impact load, making special glass of additional retention structures necessary.

The window breast height required by building regulations (depending on the maximum acceptable drop height) must be met to prevent falls from all opening windows and for story-high, large-format fixed glazing and or fully glazed doors. > Chapter Aperture components, Elements This can be achieved with a window breast, a fixed glazing element or a rail. > Fig. 8

Easily accessible areas of the exterior wall (e.g. the ground floor or windows linked by rendered balconies) usually need special measures for protection against burglary. Windows and glazed doors are at risk from being opened by simple prying tools, as normal window fittings are not burglar-proof. Protection against break-ins can be improved by installing a matching overall structure to resist burglars (frame complete with opening element, fittings and glazing), or by using safety or window grilles or opening devices.

CONTROL FUNCTIONS

When planning openings – their size, arrangement, etc. – a variety of requirements, some contradictory, must be met and combined coherently.

The aperture size affects not just the degree of view through the opening and contact with the outside world, but above all the lighting possibilities and the direct use of solar energy.

Orientation towards a point of the compass is crucially important, along with absolute size, the "aperture area" (area of opening, proportion of frame).

Increasing the aperture size means:

_ More daylight admitted
_ More radiation admitted
_ Overheating problems in summer
_ Reduced heat insulation
_ Increased need for cleaning

Arrangement within the wall surface and the aperture's geometrical shape are always linked with the room behind. Both affect the amount of light admitted, ventilation and the users' visual connections with the outside world.

>

\\ Note:
Most countries regulate the arrangement of openings in walls that face adjacent buildings, stipulating separation distances, etc. As a rule the minimum distance apart is ≥ 5 m.

\\ Important:
The following dimensions can be used as a basis for planning sightlines in living rooms (height above floor):
_ Top edge of window area ≥ 2.2 m
_ Bottom edge of window area ≥ 0.95 m
_ Width of window area ≥ 55% of room width.

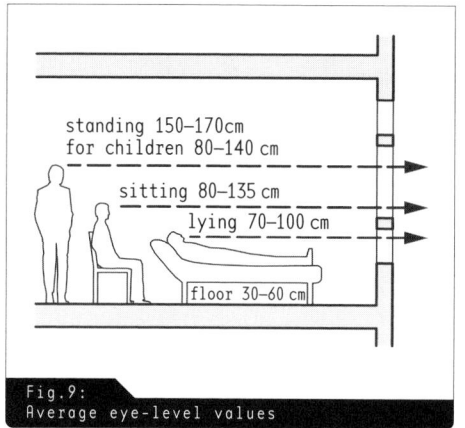

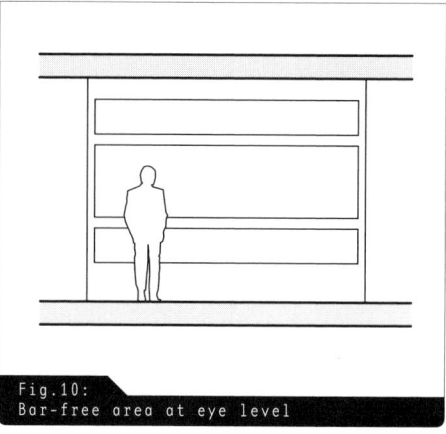

Fig.9:
Average eye-level values

Fig.10:
Bar-free area at eye level

The position of an opening relates to use both horizontally and vertically. Variants in furniture can change the horizontal relationship with openings.

On the vertical, the exterior wall is divided into the following areas:

_ Transom light (top part of the window above the transom)
_ Window light (field of vision from the interior)
_ Window breast

Sightlines

Contact with the outside world is achieved by using transparent, distortion-free and ideally color-neutral building materials such as glass or plastic. Sightlines can be opened up through the size and arrangement of the windows – e.g. by using strip windows, panoramic panes, floor-to-ceiling glazing – and also strongly defined or restricted – e.g. by using smaller openings or a precisely placed arrangement. › Fig. 9

Eye level

People's eye level when sitting or standing should be considered when placing apertures. Human proportions such as body size, field of vision, and the particular activity (sitting, standing, lying), are key factors here. The following average eye-level or sightline values can be applied for various positions:

_ approx. 150–170 cm when standing
_ approx. 80–135 cm when sitting (at work)
_ approx. 70–100 cm when lying down

› 💡

17

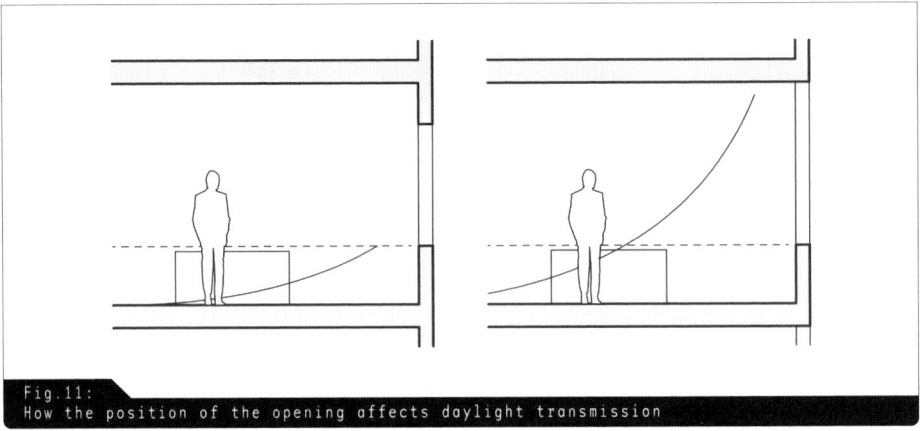

The opening area should be subdivided according to the users' activities and positions, and the visual links with the outside space on the sightline should not be impaired by placing horizontal or vertical building components directly at eye level. › Fig. 10

Visual contact with the outside world is often associated with the desire for fresh air, i.e. with being able to stand by an open window. Opening and closing mechanisms should therefore be easily accessible.

Lighting

Natural lighting is important both physiologically and in terms of energy consumption. Daily and seasonal changes in the sun's position can be seen and experienced inside through the play of light and shade and the changing color of the light. Adequate natural light is important for well-being and good for productivity at work.

Building regulations generally require one-eighth of the floor space (usable space) as the minimum proportion for openings in living rooms. This minimum value is correlated with the depth of the room. If light

○
\\ Important:
The daylight factor (D) defines the proportion
of incident light and gives the ratio of il-
lumination strengths inside and outside (dif-
fused light only) as a percentage under normal
conditions.

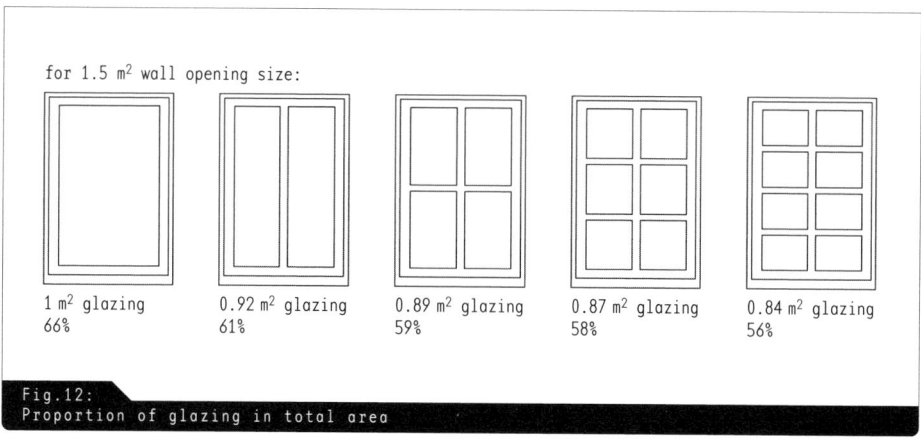

for 1.5 m² wall opening size:

| 1 m² glazing | 0.92 m² glazing | 0.89 m² glazing | 0.87 m² glazing | 0.84 m² glazing |
| 66% | 61% | 59% | 58% | 56% |

Fig.12:
Proportion of glazing in total area

enters from one side only, the amount of available light will diminish with the depth of the room.

External influences

External influences include:

_ Orientation and direction faced
_ Daily and seasonal variations
_ Lighting strength and light color
_ Shading from the immediate vicinity (vegetation, other buildings)

The position of the top edge of the aperture is important when lighting a room. The higher the window, the more light will penetrate to the back of the room. Given the same aperture area, the daylight factor will increase with the height of the top edge of the aperture above floor level. On the other hand, open areas in the window breast area (below the 0.85 m reference level) will make only a small contribution to improving incident daylight. › Fig. 11

The position of the opening in the outside wall is more important than absolute size for daylight utilization. Generally the amount of daylight penetrating through openings placed vertically in an outside wall is lower by a factor of approximately 5 than light from a horizontal opening of the same size in a flat roof. The degree of brightness actually available in a room depends on the degree of reflection from the interior surfaces, and this in turn is greatly influenced by dominant colors.

Workstations should be placed close to windows. Attention should be paid to the direction in which the light falls (to avoid people working

Fig.13:
Art Nouveau window

in their own light) and the main direction in which the user looks (usually parallel to the opening).

When lighting a room, light can be lost through the positioning of structural elements, and through dirt. Up to 40% of the window area is taken up by frames, uprights, transoms, and bars. > Figs 12 and 13

Lateral structural elements, such as protecting wall sections, and elements that protrude above the opening (canopies, roof overhangs, balconies) restrict incident light and the way it is distributed in the room. The surfaces of such opaque structural elements should thus be as reflective as possible, i.e. they should be painted in light colors to throw the light back. Natural light can be exploited better by placing light-directing systems in front of openings and using highly reflective materials as ceiling cladding, to take light into the depths of the space.

Using solar energy

Sunlight is important for rooms in which leisure time is spent. Sunbeams coming in through glazed apertures can also be used to complement the building's heating system through the "greenhouse effect".

If combined with the spaces immediately behind them, openings are simple collection and storage systems. Four important parameters determine the proportion of solar energy that can be used directly: climatic and local factors, orientation in a particular direction, the aperture's angle of inclination, and freedom from shade.

In Central Europe, solar radiation is available but does not clearly coincide with heating needs on either a daily or a seasonal level. In a house with good heat insulation, up to one-third of the heat required can be supplied by solar energy if direct sunlight is exploited via south-facing surfaces in the heating period. If openings face east or west (receiving particularly intensive sunlight in summer), care should be taken to ensure that the aperture proportion is not above about 40%, in order to maintain thermal equilibrium.

> ☉ The amount of radiation admitted is in direct proportion to the aperture area, so large glazed areas can cause overheating.

Exposure to sunlight, aperture size, heat needed and interior thermal storage materials should be in balance. Even in the heating period, openings taking up over 50% of the available area are not required. Provided that sunshading precautions are taken (e.g. projecting structural components), it is possible to achieve comfortable interior temperatures even

> ◖ without cooling systems.

Exploitable solar gain is additionally restricted by structural and user-related influences. Thus it makes sense to choose narrow frame sections and to use filigree subdivisions. Net or other curtains also reduce solar gain. Internal screening and antiglare systems further reduce the amount of solar radiation stored.

Actually exploitable solar radiation can be reduced by almost half the theoretical starting value as a result of building features, and can decrease further to one-third as a result of user-related influences.

Ventilation After lighting, ventilation is most important aperture function. Ventilation is a basic condition for user wellbeing and health, and for protecting

---

☉

\\ Important:
In offices with a high proportion of glazing, overheating in combination with internal thermal loads (artificial light, office equipment, people) means that a lot of cooling is needed.

◖

\\ Note:
Solar gain refers to solar energy entering the building via windows and other transparent/translucent structural components. It helps to raise the temperature of the building and the air in the rooms, and thus reduce heating requirements. But only a proportion of the solar gain can be exploited, while the rest is dissipated in the surrounding area.

the building stock. Ventilation means exchanging the air in the room for fresh air. This traditionally happens via windows in the exterior wall area (desirable air change), or via joints between opening and window element or antiglare devices or opening leaves (undesirable air change).

Such air change is caused by interior and exterior pressure differences, and is called free or natural ventilation (also shock ventilation). Exchange of the internal air helps to supply the room with fresh air, remove water vapor, odors and exhaled CO_2, and contributes considerably to comfort levels.

The window's area and the way it opens determine the degree of air change. Additional open windows (e.g. in an opposite wall), how far interior doors are open and the position of devices like roller or slatted blinds increase ventilation. As users behave in different ways, air change rates of 0.5 to 1/h are recommended. Air speed affects comfort as well as air change. The upper limit indoors is 0.2 m/s.

Windows that can be opened individually have the advantage that the fresh air admitted can be regulated directly by the user. Open windows should not knock against other structural elements (e.g. sunshading, antiglare or screening systems, wall, columns) or restrict the use of the interior. If windows are arranged on one side only, rooms are considered as suitable for natural ventilation if the room depth does not exceed the dimension of the clear opening height by a factor of more than 2.5.

Room ventilation is not necessarily linked to windows. In triple thermopane glazing in particular, or large-format panes, the weight of the fittings can make it preferable to separate a well-insulated, light ventilation flap from a fixed glazing element. › Fig. 14

\\ Note:
The air change rate n in the unit (1/h) indicates how often the room or building volume is changed within an hour.
Example: n = 10/h:
10 times the room or building volume is changed in one hour.

\\ Important:
Air change (AC)

Window positions	AC per hour
Window and door closed	0.1 to 0.3
Window tilted, blinds closed	0.3 to 1.5
Window tilted	0.8 to 4
Window half open	5 to 10
Window fully open	9 to 15
Opposite windows	
Intermediate doors fully open	up to 40

Fig.14:
Glazing element with opaque
ventilation flap

Window ventilation raises a number of problems caused by user behavior. Regular ventilation is often neglected, and manual ventilation does not produce sufficient air change. As the flow of air cannot be controlled, this causes increased ventilation heat losses in winter and the need for additional cooling in winter.

Ventilation heat losses become more important for buildings' energy budgets as exterior wall construction improves in terms of heat technology. An inappropriate approach to ventilation can be avoided by a controlled air supply, but can lead to the loss of individual regulation. Mechanical inward and outward ventilation systems are installed in passive buildings in particular.

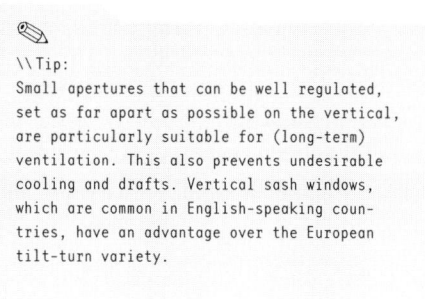

\\ Tip:
Small apertures that can be well regulated,
set as far apart as possible on the vertical,
are particularly suitable for (long-term)
ventilation. This also prevents undesirable
cooling and drafts. Vertical sash windows,
which are common in English-speaking countries, have an advantage over the European
tilt-turn variety.

Fig.15:
Geometrical edge design

In many (primarily older) buildings there is additional air change through structural joints. Joint ventilation cannot be controlled and does not distribute or remove air evenly. Joints can also cause damage to structural components by accumulated condensation. But this aspect is becoming less relevant as seals improve and interfaces can be made completely airtight in new buildings.

EDGES

Openings are bordered by structural elements that perform different functions according to position. A structure based on right angles, resulting in the first place from the building materials used and their modular dimensions, is not essential. Adaptations can affect daylight input, the view outside, and the direct use of solar energy.

In construction with thick walls in particular, the aperture is also the space between the outer, weatherproof skin and the internal surface wall, which can be shaped three-dimensionally according to the position of the window.

Energy-saving building and more modern approaches have also meant that walls are no longer becoming less thick in "modern" structural vocabulary: because of increased heat insulation requirements and the resultant greater insulation thicknesses, walls are getting thicker again. So the way edges are handled is once again topical.

Wall thickness

Wall thickness and reveal design, the light admitted, and solar energy use are all affected, with the same aperture area. In addition, building

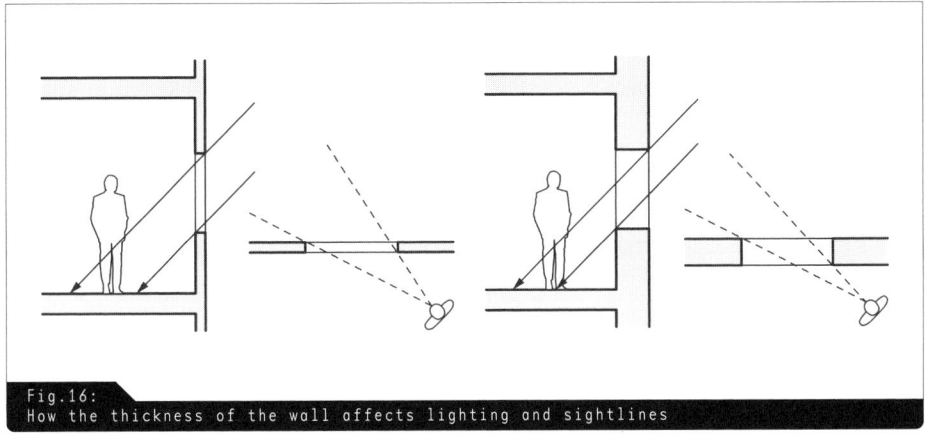

type and construction method also affect sightlines from inside to outside, by expanding or restricting the visual links. › Figs 15 and 16

In non-loadbearing curtain facades, which have narrower wall super-structures and thus considerably less depth of shade, the dimensions of posts and rails extending into the room have to be taken into account, as well as the thickness of the glazing.

Geometrical design

The depths of the edges depend on the structure of the wall. The design is associated with the rebate on the elements closing the aperture (e.g. windows or fixed glazing).

The edges can be beveled, in order to increase the amount of light admitted in the case of small apertures, or to make them seem larger. These (window) incisions can be arranged diagonally facing outwards or inwards. The amount of daylight admitted can also be increased by painting the edges of the reveal a light, highly reflective color.

The edge of the aperture can be changed all the way round or individually, symmetrically or asymmetrically. Regardless of the material quality of the exterior wall, the beveled edges can be in exposed masonry or can be appropriately rendered, in concrete or natural stone.

Outward-facing beveling

Beveling facing outwards in the lintel area enlarges the proportion of zenith light admitted to the interior. A clearly inclined sill improves rainwater drainage and gives an enhanced sense of connection with the outside

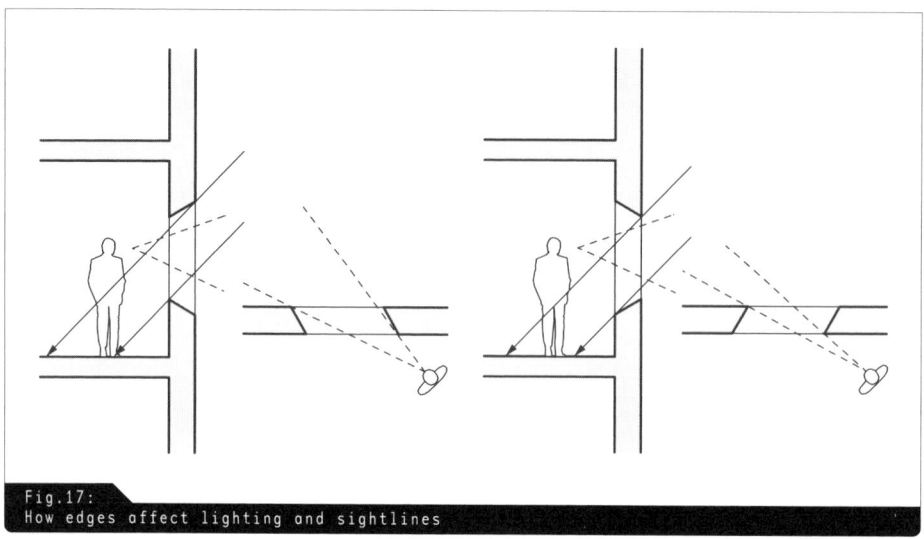

Fig.17:
How edges affect lighting and sightlines

world, especially in multi-story buildings; and a window breast can also act as a sightscreen. › Fig. 17

Inward-facing beveling

Reveals widened on the inside reduce the light density contrast between wall and aperture and thus prevent glare. The straight edge reinforces the silhouette effect. There is a relatively small edge between the opening, toplit on the room side, and the dark wall. In case of a cloudless sky and areas exposed to the sun, the beveling creates a medium-bright transitional zone. Depending on the reveal depth and angle, there is little or no glare.

Make the window frame a deep, splayed edge: about a foot wide and splayed at about 50 to 60 degrees to the plane of the window, so that the gentle gradient of daylight gives a smooth transition between the light of the window and the dark of the inner wall." (Christopher Alexander et al., *A Pattern Language*, Oxford University Press, New York 1977, p. 1055)

In contrast to historical examples, many contemporary buildings come up with a number of asymmetrical solutions. These create a special sense of closeness to local climatic conditions or features of the urban situation. › Figs 18 and 19

Care should be taken when finishing edges geometrically so that they relate correctly to the size of the aperture and its ratio to the wall area. Staggering or stepping individual structural elements or offsetting edges

Fig.18:
One edge beveled

Fig.19:
Two edges beveled

makes the wall look sculpture externally. This effect is further enhanced by the resultant play of light and shade, the different surface materials, and the varied colors. The depth of the edges can also be increased, but not reduced, by shifting other structural elements off the plane of the outer skin (jambs or extended reveal boards). › Chapter Aperture components, Elements

Even though there is little quantified material available about the interplay of aperture size, edge design, light admission or solar energy use, it opens up the aperture planning repertoire enormously on the design plane.

CONTROL DEVICES
Control devices are added to apertures for planned manual or mechanical control of climate and weather effects on the space. Structural devices like this can be used to regulate the degree of permeability and thus air quality, as well as the temperature and moisture levels between indoor

\\ Example:
Examples of geometrically accentuated aperture edges can be found in buildings by the Frankfurt architect Christoph Mäckler, and the Stuttgart practice Lederer Ragnarsdóttir Oei.

Fig.20:
Shutters with movable slots

and outdoor space, according to the time of day or year, or can provide full or complete shade for radiation or transmission. Several such devices can be combined and used together according to the movement mechanism and the amount of strength required.

The search is also on, while aperture areas are being enlarged, for materials and structural elements that can be used to influence the extent of the desired permeability. Early versions of these devices were made of skins, fabric or paper. These were later followed by (wooden) shutters that could be turned or slid, or covered with semi-transparent organic materials. These simple wooden shutters have developed into a wide variety of movable elements as existing ones have been refined and new systems devised. › Fig. 20

Control devices can also be operated mechanically. Sensors make it possible to control the system automatically, in line with the weather. Here it makes sense for users to be able to override the system individually if they wish. Comfort levels and energy consumption can be optimized by combining various elements or principles.

Positioning   Positioning such control devices affects their functional context directly. This applies to their:

_ Position in relation to the opening (top/middle/bottom/one or more sides)

_ Position on the outer wall (on the outside, away from the opening/ on the outside/built into the window plane/inside)

Functional
properties
Control devices differ in their technical and material design, and particularly in the way they are operated and the degree of variability; in this case the extent to which the opening is enlarged. In addition, the nature and direction of the movement have a part to play.

A wide variety of finishes are available in the familiar systems. There are three ways of looking at the main typological features:

_ Permeability
_ Movement (by the element)
_ Packed size

Permeability
The nature and extent of permeability for light, air and heat has a crucial effect on the qualities required of a control device. Intermediate positions can be set between open and closed. The desired degree of permeability must then be set (e.g. from fully open to a narrow slit).

Movement
Control devices can be categorized as movable or constructed to move. This can apply in terms of time: movable temporarily, but fixed, i.e. as secondary double glazing or a window shutter, or permanently movable like a folding shutter or roller blind.

In this book control devices are treated as permanently movable elements. There are also systems that do not move at all (e.g. switchable special glass, gasochromic or electrochromic glass). › Chapter Window components, Special glass

Control devices can be assembled from different components. They can move in different ways, and create different conditions and variable degrees of permeability.

Packed size
The packed size, i.e. change in relative dimensions, is crucial to using control devices. It can remain unchanged (as in a hinged shutter), reduced (as in a folding shutter or – even more clearly – in the case of slatted blinds, where the packed height is about 6 to 10% of the maximum area covered), and directly affects the way they are handled.

Nature and
direction of
movement
Types of movement are often a combination of movement principles. Combined with direction, they offer a variety of possibilities. Comfort can be regulated efficiently when it is possible to respond to the effects of

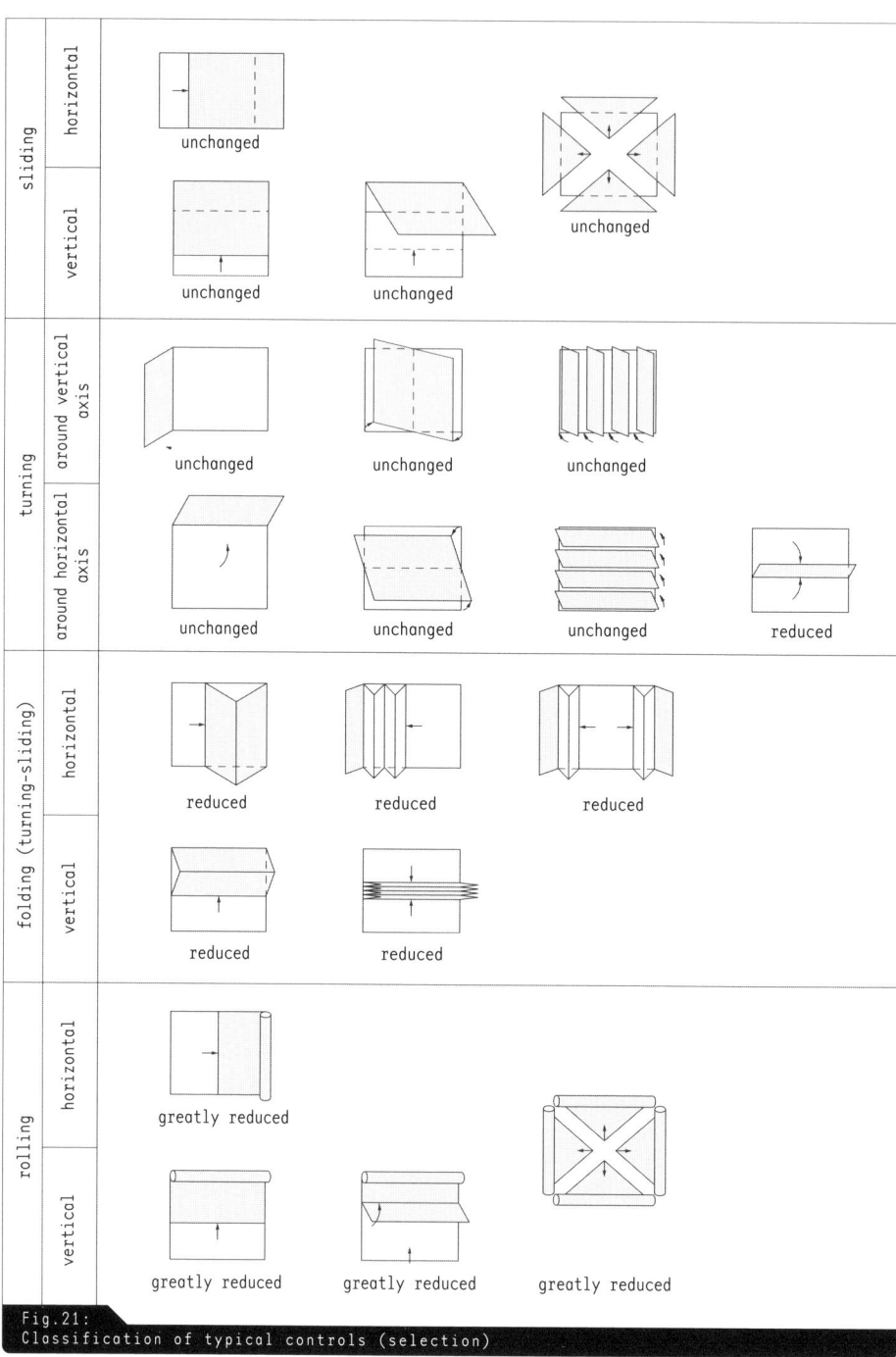

Fig.21:
Classification of typical controls (selection)

30

light, sound and heat technology independently of each other. Movement can be

- Around the vertical axis (rotation, roller shutters)
- Around the horizontal axis (rotation, horizontal slat)
- Complete change of place without changing the element (translation, sliding shutter)
- Complete change of place and of the element (transformation, roller blind)

The kinds of movement can also be categorized in terms of operation and the amount of space needed with reference to the facade plane – usually outside/inside and top/bottom:

- Turning: opening inwards/outwards
- Folding: opening inwards/outwards
- Sliding: horizontally (to the right/left/vertically (upwards, downwards) › Fig. 21

Construction types

The simplest control device for closing apertures is the shutter, which is commonly made of wood as the material is readily available, works well, and is easy to handle. There are also examples in natural stone and, since the 19th century, metal as well in many places. Shutters were used as an alternative to windows at first, and then in addition to them, from the 15th century onwards.

Movement and fixing types

Control devices can be categorized by movement and fixing type:

- <u>Sliding shutters</u> (sliding horizontally), placed at the side of small apertures, set on tracks inside or outside › Fig. 22
- <u>Dropped/raised shutters</u> (sliding vertically), set above or below the aperture, usually set into the wall structure

\\ Example:
Window shutters can be used to show the device's increasing sophistication and increasingly complex construction. Starting with the opaque timber shutter, the panels then acquired translucent or transparent apertures to provide a minimum of light and view outside. In about 1700, the flat boards were replaced with fixed diagonal slots. They later become movable manually: a strip of wood or a metal bar could be used to adjust the amount of light permeating. There are early examples with the shutter divided into different functional areas, so that the light admitted, the view through, ventilation, and privacy screening can be adjusted independently.

Fig.22:
Horizontal sliding element in light-weight metal

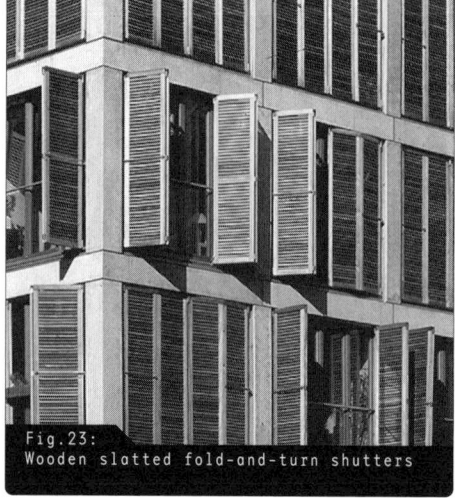

Fig.23:
Wooden slatted fold-and-turn shutters

_ <u>Hinged shutters</u> (moved by turning), fixed on hinges to the side of the aperture; the variant is vertically slatted shutters › Fig. 20

_ <u>Box shutters</u> (moved by folding and tilting), fixed on hinges above or below the aperture

_ <u>Folding shutters</u> (moved by a combination of sliding and turning), fixed on side hinges › Figs 23 and 24

_ <u>Roller shutters</u> (narrow slats, strung on strings or chains) or (membrane) roller blinds (moved by rolling), fastened above the aperture, partly let into the wall structure

_ <u>Slatted or Venetian blinds</u> (narrow slats, fastened together on strings; moved by a combination of sliding and turning), fitted above the aperture, partly let into the wall structure › Fig. 25

Control devices are available in almost all the usual construction materials. If many combinations of individual components with different movement mechanisms are involved, care should be taken to ensure that these do not prevent each other from working properly.

Element sizes The element size or cross section depends on the dimensions and movement of the control device. Hence upright formats are appropriate in terms of handling and the effect the load makes on fittings and support structure for sliding and folding shutters, horizontal formats for box shutters. Sliding shutters can jam very easily if the proportions of the long and narrow sides are extreme. Care should be taken over the span width for linear systems such as slatted and roller blinds to prevent bending.

Fig.24:
Opaque wooden fold-and-turn shutters

Fig.25:
Lightweight metal Venetian blinds

Practical ex-
ample: shading
devices
It is important when choosing a control device to be familiar with the interplay between the effect of the weather and the principle on which the device works. When providing protection from the sun (shade for the aperture), it is necessary to respond to the different climatic conditions in each case, and the changing daily and seasonal position of the sun throughout the year.

Various principles can be identified by taking the provision of shade for a south-facing aperture as an example:

_ Complete, direct covering for the aperture: this blocks visual contact with the outside world, so artificial light will be needed in the room.
_ Semi-transparent structures (perforations, expanded metal, etc.): extensive shading allows some contact with the outside world and admits some light. › Fig. 26

Slotted
structure
It is more effective to divide the area up with an accumulation of small elements in a slatted structure: the slats can be adjusted as the sun moves – and still provide the same amount of view outside. The best approach uses non-linked, separately controlled systems. This provides shade and a possible view outside on the sightline. Incident daylight can then independently be directed in the upper section of the window. These systems provide good protection from the sun, while allowing natural lighting and visual contact, which can be optimized by using semi-transparent slats. › Fig. 27

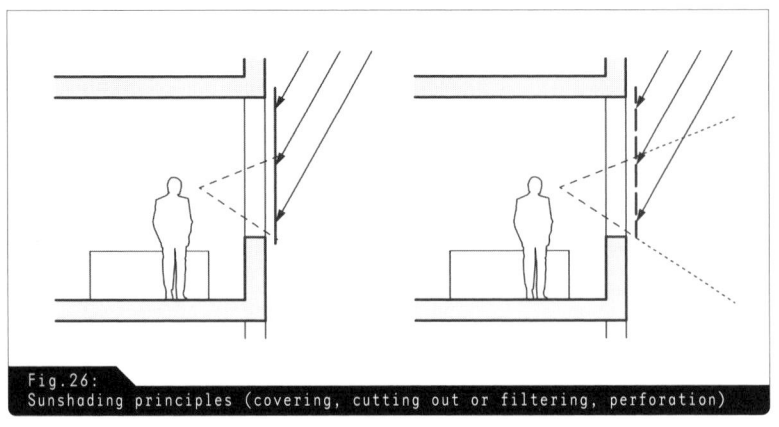

Fig.26:
Sunshading principles (covering, cutting out or filtering, perforation)

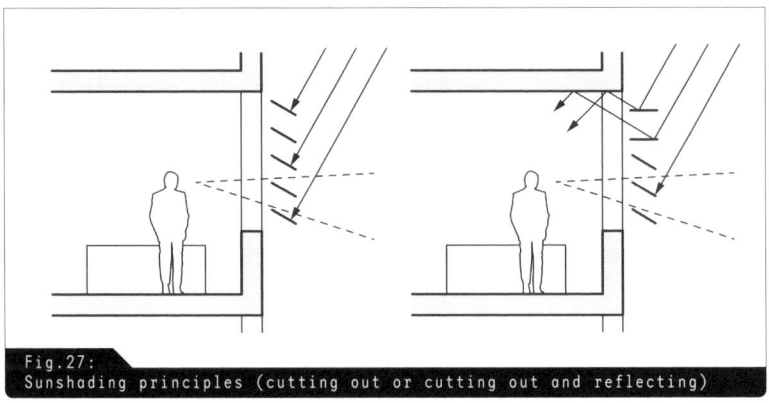

Fig.27:
Sunshading principles (cutting out or cutting out and reflecting)

Positioning principles

Two positioning principles can be applied to slatted structures, based on the direction in which the window faces and the associated position of the sun:

_ Horizontal slats prevent sunshine at a steep angle on the south side from penetrating the space. The shallower the radiation angle (east and west side), the more comprehensive the shading will need to be.

_ If apertures face east and west, vertical slats are used to prevent transmission.

Shading is provided, but it is still possible to see out. › Figs 28–30

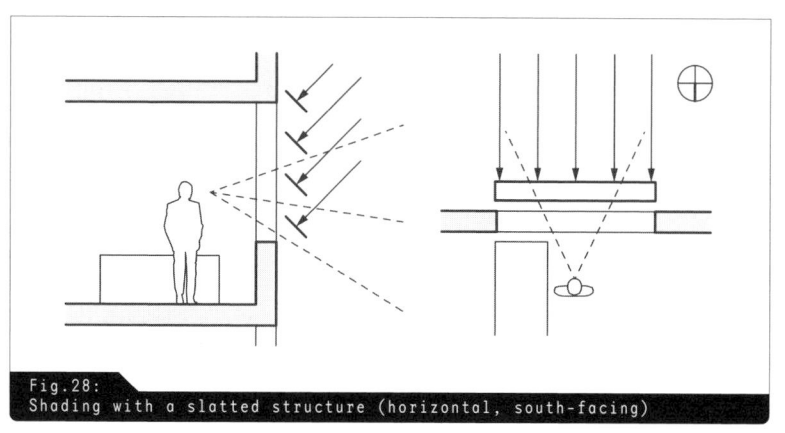

Fig.28:
Shading with a slatted structure (horizontal, south-facing)

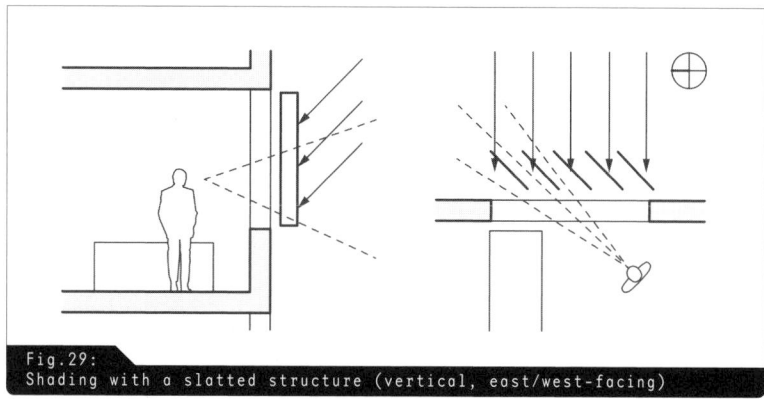

Fig.29:
Shading with a slatted structure (vertical, east/west-facing)

Fig.30:
Lightweight vertical metal slat

APERTURE COMPONENTS

ELEMENTS

Lintel

The topmost element of a wall opening is the lintel. It spans the opening, and transfers loads into the loadbearing wall cross sections at the side, the reveals. The simplest lintel is a beam that can carry a bending load (e.g. wood, reinforced concrete, steel). The aperture size is limited by length limits specific to the material and the maximum admissible deflection of the beam. Pressure-loaded lintel constructions are traditionally used in masonry building in particular (e.g. horizontal arches). The supports have to absorb both vertical and horizontal loads from the arch structure.

Reinforced concrete lintels can be cast on site at the same time as the ceiling, or supplied as a prefabricated lintel. The range of prefabricated lintels includes reinforced concrete units and brick shells with concrete-clad steel reinforcement, U-shell prefabricated lintels, and roller blind lintels.

Sunshading systems

For particular building orientations and exterior wall concepts a sunshading system (e.g. roller blinds, curtaining) may have to be built into the lintel or attached to the outside. Integrating them into the lintel area can affect shell geometry and thus the protective function of the external wall.

Apertures can also be closed flush with the ceiling, without a lintel. This makes the interior look more generous and admits more daylight. Where necessary, the edge of the ceiling slab is reinforced to span the opening.

Window breast

The bottom of an aperture can take the form of a window breast. Solid masonry sections or fixed window element must be high enough to prevent people from falling out. According to the position of the window in the outside wall, a horizontal internal covering, a windowsill, should be provided; this is particularly important outside.

Radiators are often fitted inside the space in the window breast area; these reduce the amount of cold air flowing down from the glass panes,

---

\\ Note:
For more information on static systems, loadbearing behavior and supports see *Basics Loadbearing Systems* by Alfred Meistermann, Birkhäuser Publishers, 2007.

among other things. The customary radiator niches must not significantly detract from the statical efficiency of the wall cross section and the wall's heat permeation resistance.

As a rule, French windows do not have a breast. The bottom of the door must be adequately sealed, which is usually achieved by adding a threshold. It is possible to provide threshold-free access to the outdoor space or a balcony by using grids or gutters. The balcony or terrace must be fitted with protection against falling if it is more than one meter above the ground.

Rebate

The rebate is the shallow connection between the window frame and the shell of the building. We distinguish between › Fig. 31

(a) Window with internal rebate › Fig. 33
(b) Window without rebate
(c) Window with external rebate.

Independently of this, the window can be placed on various planes. › Fig. 32

(d) Flush with the interior
(e) Centrally in the reveal
(f) Flush with the exterior

The insulation layer must always come right up to the window. There are usually rebates on three sides, in each reveal and in the lintel area. Windows with a reveal – central positioning is most common, with an interior rebate – make it possible to create a chicane between the shell and the window frame, while for windows without rebate the requirements for a joint (sealing, insulating, fixing) must be fulfilled within the depth of the frame.

\\ Example:
Maximum acceptable drop height
If windows open, the required window breast height must be met with solid window breasts or fixed glazing elements to prevent people from falling out. For opening French windows there must be additional protection against falling inside or outside, depending on the direction of opening, e.g. in the form of a railing.
Breast or railing heights depend on the height and purpose of the building. Solid window breasts should be ≥ 80–90 cm high up to the 12 m drop height (except on the ground floor), above 90–110 cm. Window breasts may be lower if an additional guardrail is provided.

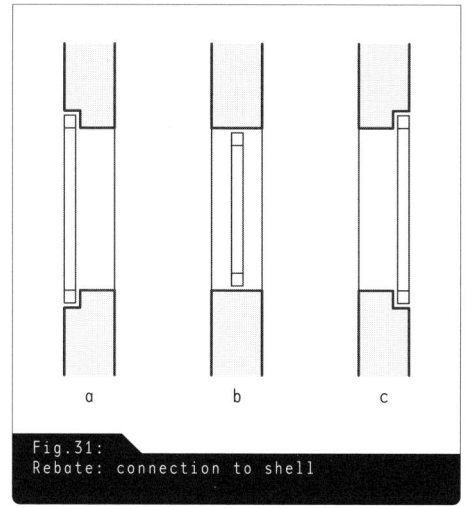

Fig.31:
Rebate: connection to shell

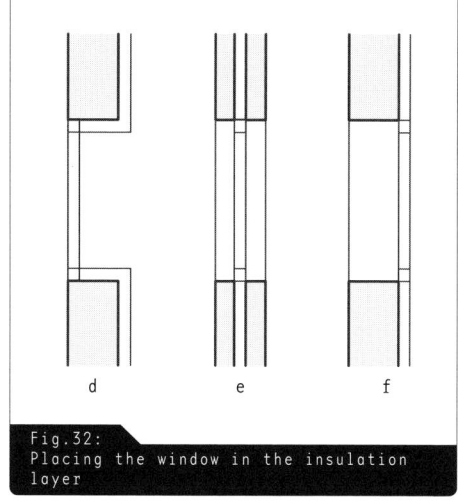

Fig.32:
Placing the window in the insulation layer

External rebate

Reveals with exterior rebates are traditionally found in particularly stormy areas (e.g. North Sea Coast). Wind pressure means that the outward-opening windows – and the window as a whole – benefit from being pressed against the seals and rebates.

Today, the fitting of the windows is the key criterion for the type of rebate. For multi-story buildings in particular, it is possible to fit windows from the outside and replace window elements from outside if they are damaged, using scaffolding or lifting devices. If elements are large or particularly heavy it can make sense to create an exterior rebate to assist lifting devices (crane).

If a window is mounted flush with the exterior, frames, glass and connecting joints are particularly exposed. Joints have to be realized with

\\ Note:
A chicane is the term for a geometrically shaped structural element, e.g. with a rebate or groove, a built-in obstacle in the wall structure to prevent water penetrating directly.

\\ Important:
Insulation layer – rebate
Windows should be placed within the facade insulation layer, to avoid heat bridges. The rebate also prevents precipitation from penetrating, through the principles of chicane and overlapping.

Fig.33:
Internal rebate covering the fixed frame

particular care. In terms of building physics, it is difficult to fit a window flush with the exterior even with an external rebate (peripheral joints as chicane), as the dew point is shifted a long way outwards in the window reveal area and heat bridges can be formed. This requires interior insulation of reveal and lintel where necessary. On the inside, it is possible to realize a flush transition between the reveal and the glazing in the case of fixed-glazed windows with an external rebate.

Internal rebate   In the case of an internal rebate, the window can usually be fitted from the interior without any additional effort and replaced in case of damage. The frame is pressed against the rebate from the inside and is set back in the outside wall by the depth of the rebate. The breadth of view of the window frame in the lintel area and at the reveals depends on overlapping, and can be reduced to the opening frame profile. › Fig. 33

Internal rebates offer a higher degree of safety, as the rebate overlaps the frame and the rebate joint can be realized as a chicane. The window can be fitted flush with the interior wall. Similarly to the exterior flush fitting, counter-measures must be taken against position-related heat bridges (e.g. interior insulation or insulation for the reveal).

Without rebate   If the wall aperture is realized without a rebate, this simplifies work on the shell in the first place. But greater demands are made on the joints, which have to be both wind- and vaporproof, and also free of heat bridges, but – unlike fitting approaches with rebates – only the depth of the window profile is available for this.

As long as the window is fitted within the insulation layer, or the insulation is taken to the window in the reveal area, the position of the window within the thickness of the wall can be chosen freely (flush outside, flush inside, central). The window frame is visible from both the inside and the outside over almost its full width. The bottom of a window is usually finished without a rebate, in order to meet the functional and geometrical demands of the jointing process.

Vertical loads from the window element are transferred into the loadbearing wall cross sections. Precipitation water collects along the windows and has to be deflected outwards at the bottom, e.g. by providing a sill. The wall cross section – for additional-leaf constructions the insulation in particular – is protected against damp. In the case of rear ventilated wall constructions the bottom of the window must also allow free ventilation. › Fig. 57, page 71

On the inside, the coverings (for windows with breasts) and the floor fittings (for French windows) must be attached to the bottom frame section. In addition, waterproofing seals must be fitted at the bottom of French windows in conformity with directives (e.g. flat roof directives).

BASIC CONSTRUCTIONS

Openings in the vertical component of the envelope system – the facade – are usually closed by doors and windows. These combine opening and lighting functions with the protective function of the wall. Window frames standardized by manufacturing and profile configuration are fitted into different wall constructions.

\\ Note:
French windows
The waterproofing should be attached 15 cm above the surface covering or gravel to prevent weather-related water penetration above the door or French window threshold, for example if drains are blocked or precipitation water freezes. Favorable local conditions can make it possible to reduce the attachment height, provided that water can run off without difficulty at all times (e.g. by placing a gutter outside the window aperture). But the minimum attachment height of 5 cm should adhered to even then.

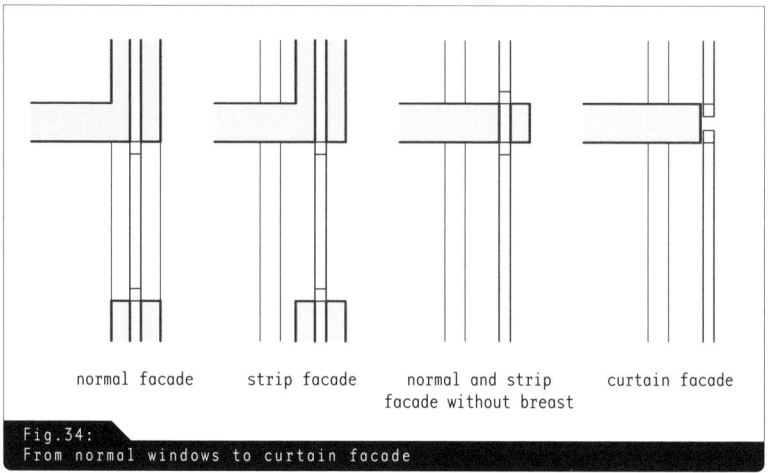

normal facade   strip facade   normal and strip   curtain facade
facade without breast

Fig.34:
From normal windows to curtain facade

Normal windows

In the normal form for windows, the openings finish at the top with a lintel, at the sides with <u>reveals</u> and at the bottom a <u>window breast</u> between them and the wall cross sections. Such windows can be combined to form continuous or <u>strip windows</u>. Here the side connections within the strip of windows consists of window elements (<u>visible frames</u>), with tops and bottoms of the normal kind.

Curtain wall facades

In curtain or window wall facades, element joints must be created at the top and the bottom. This leads to larger facade elements consisting of different window units. Vertical <u>posts</u> and horizontal <u>rails</u> articulate and subdivide multi-member window elements. › Figs 34 and 35

Aperture size

The desired aperture size directly influences the construction and material quality of the facade. Wall construction and formats define each other. Tall, narrow apertures are appropriate in masonry walls. Wide openings need high lintels and reinforcement in the reveal area. Cast reinforced concrete walls tend to be statically overdefined (the loadbearing capacity of the wall can be additionally increased with reinforcement that is invisible from the outside). This means that the openings can be enlarged correspondingly. In skeleton construction the opening can be taken as far as the columns and beams (walls and ceilings in crosswall construction), the dimensions of which are determined by statical requirements. › Fig. 36

If wide spans have to be tackled or the fixed glazing is high, the wide window sections can be replaced with narrower clamping strip sections. Opening windows have to be fitted with their own frames in this case. All

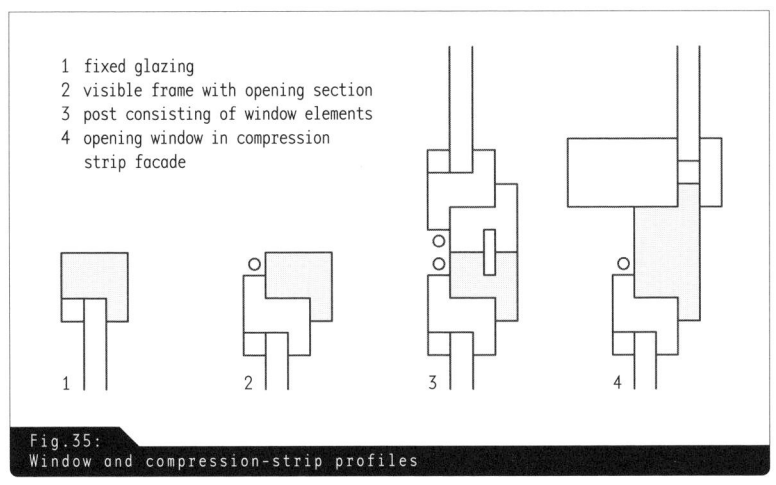

1 fixed glazing
2 visible frame with opening section
3 post consisting of window elements
4 opening window in compression
  strip facade

Fig.35:
Window and compression-strip profiles

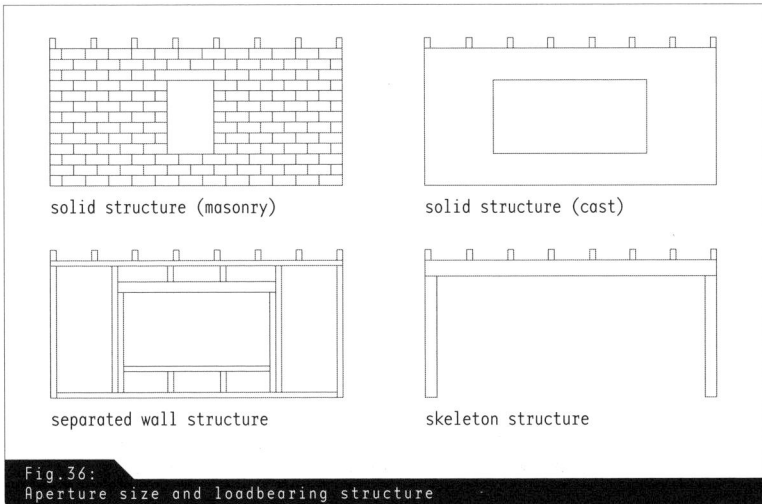

solid structure (masonry)

solid structure (cast)

separated wall structure

skeleton structure

Fig.36:
Aperture size and loadbearing structure

the major manufacturers offer window and clamping strip sections in various materials and a wide range of dimensions, some of them standardized.

› Chapter Window components, Frames

Connection to wall

The way a window is connected to a wall requires different approaches at the sides, top and bottom. The connection area is most heavily loaded in the window breast area, and in the lintel area the need to build

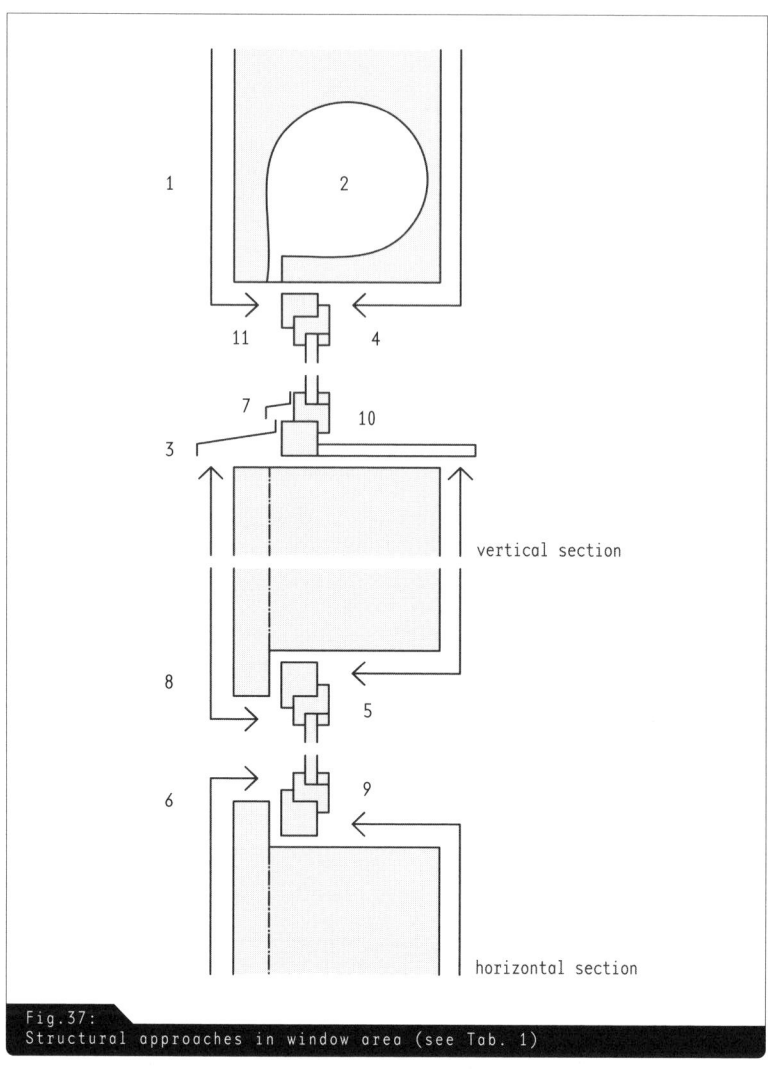

vertical section

horizontal section

Fig. 37:
Structural approaches in window area (see Tab. 1)

in roller blinds and sun protection systems makes clear geometrical solutions difficult. › Fig. 37 and Tab. 1

General structural principles such as direct load dispersion, continuous insulation, adequate tolerances, seals between different structural elements, chicanes, and overlaps are addressed in specific strategies for constructing the window joints.

Tab.1:
Aperture planning principles (see Fig. 37)

		side	top	bottom
1	Load dispersed via opening, lintel		x	
2	Integrating control devices	x	x	(x)
3	Exterior drip edge		x	x
4	Tolerance, seal between frame and wall	x	x	x
5	Fixing the window (tension-free)	x	(x)	
6	Taking the exterior cladding up to the window element	x	(x)	(x)
7	Heavy rain seal outside	x		x
8	Rebate for the window element	(x)	(x)	
9	Taking the interior cladding up to the window element	(x)	(x)	
10	Change of material for the reveal (sill, framing)	(x)	(x)	x
11	Insulation in the reveal area	(x)	(x)	(x)

x always
(x) possible

WINDOW COMPONENTS

> › Chapter Frames and Figs 38–40

OPENING TYPES

Windows that can be opened operate in a number of different ways.

Turn, tilt, tilt-turn window

The turn window can be opened inwards or outwards on a vertical axis, and the tilt-turn window can also be tilted inwards on the lower horizontal axis. For ease of use, turn, tilt and tilt-turn windows usually open inwards. One variant is the turn-fold window, which can open inwards out outwards. › Fig. 41 It is also important to establish whether the window is hinged on the right or the left.

Top-hung or flap window

Flap windows open outwards. The turning axis is placed horizontally at the top, to prevent rain coming in when the flap is open. › Fig. 42

The rebates for opening windows and frames are stepped on the outside, corresponding to the direction of opening. › Fig. 43 The upper joint between the frame and the opening window is susceptible to heavy rain. A weather bar is usually fitted so that precipitation water can run off and not down the facade.

Sliding, lift-and-slide windows

Horizontal sliding windows slide sideways and usually open on the inside of the fixed element for reasons of sealing tightness. Lift-and-slide windows are raised vertically before sliding, which makes them easier to operate.

Vertical sliding window often open upwards in the case of two-part windows, but also downwards in the case of large windows without breasts. › Fig. 43 Here the sliding sections can be lowered into the floor (e.g. into the basement story), so that they can be stepped out of at ground level.

\\ Note:

The way windows open should be shown in the working plan views on a scale of 1:15: turning movements are drawn in as unbroken lines in exterior views (opening outwards), or dashed lines (opening inwards), and sliding movements as arrows in the direction of opening. When dimensioning the opening on ground plans the height of the opening is entered as well as width, with the width figure placed above the dimension line and the height figure below it.

Further information on plan presentation can be found in *Basics Technical Drawing* by Bert Bielefeld and Isabella Skiba, Birkhäuser Publishers, 2007.

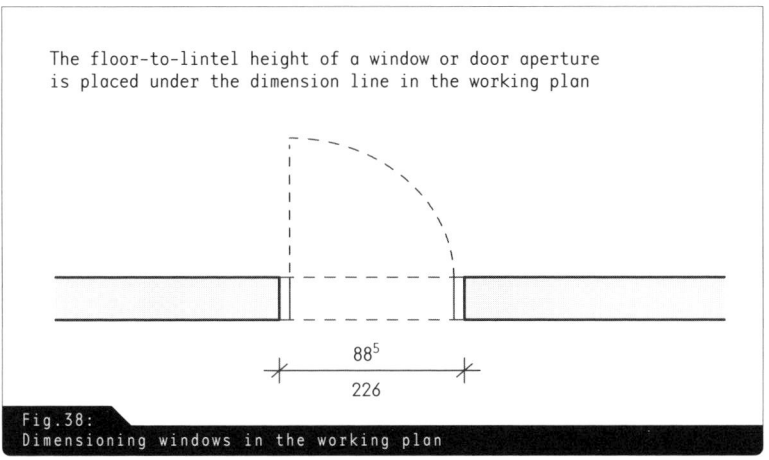

The floor-to-lintel height of a window or door aperture is placed under the dimension line in the working plan

88^5

226

Fig.38:
Dimensioning windows in the working plan

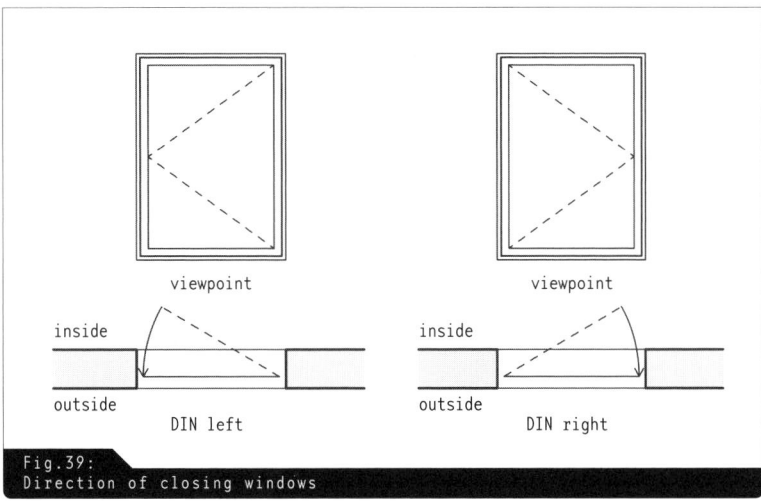

viewpoint

viewpoint

inside

inside

outside

outside

DIN left

DIN right

Fig.39:
Direction of closing windows

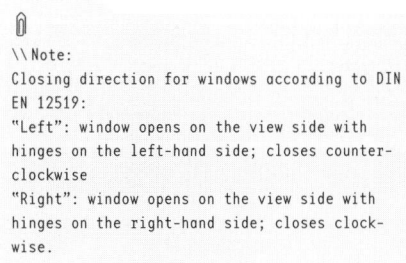

\\Note:
Closing direction for windows according to DIN EN 12519:
"Left": window opens on the view side with hinges on the left-hand side; closes counter-clockwise
"Right": window opens on the view side with hinges on the right-hand side; closes clockwise.

47

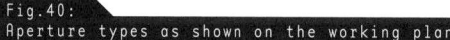

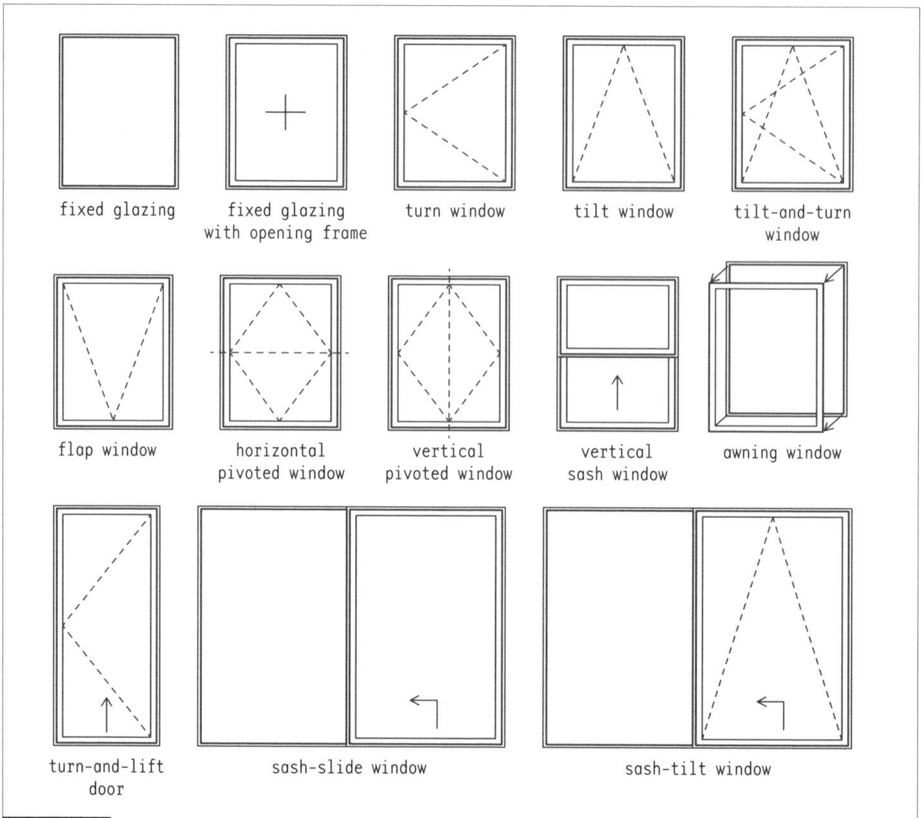
fixed glazing
fixed glazing with opening frame
turn window
tilt window
tilt-and-turn window
flap window
horizontal pivoted window
vertical pivoted window
vertical sash window
awning window
turn-and-lift door
sash-slide window
sash-tilt window

Fig.40:
Aperture types as shown on the working plan

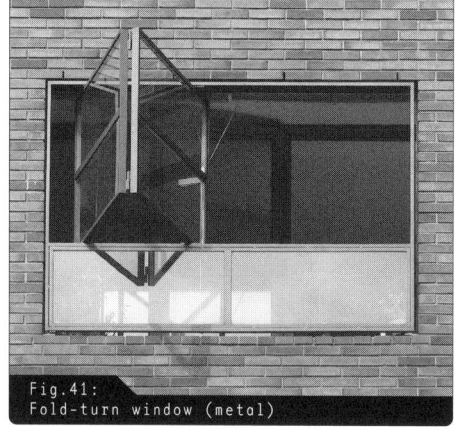

Fig.41:
Fold-turn window (metal)

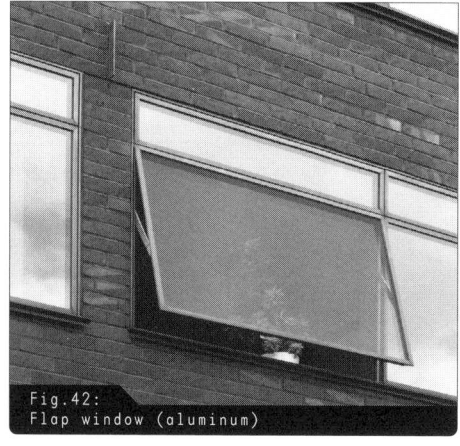

Fig.42:
Flap window (aluminum)

Abb.43:
Vertical sash window (wood)

Lift-slide-tilt windows
Lift-slide-tilt windows can also be tilted inwards around the horizontal axis, which greatly increases the complexity of the fittings, and the amount of space they occupy.

Horizontal pivoted window
A horizontal pivoted window turns horizontally around its central axis, i.e. the outside of the pane can be turned into the interior, which makes cleaning the glass easier, among other things. The centrally placed pivotal hinge means that the profiling and the sealing rebates are offset. Only half the window aperture is accessible as a free cross section at any time. This is relevant if the window is intended to be part of an escape route. Windows of this type were commonly used in the 1950s and 1960s, but are quite rarely fitted today, mainly because of sealing problems around the pivot.

Vertical pivoted window
The vertical pivoted window uses the same principle, and has raised the same problems. The opening window turns around the central axis in a vertical direction.

Slatted window
A series of small flaps, or vertically or horizontally pivoted slats, is called a slatted window. If each of the slats has its own frame, the proportion of frame to the glazed area is relatively high. The dimensions of the individual slats fall between at least 200 × 100 mm, or a maximum of 2000 × 400 mm. Element sizes run from at least 300 × 150 mm to a maximum of 2000 x 3000 mm.

Awning window
Awning windows are pushed in front of the facade plane by a scissor device, thus providing excellent ventilation: cold air can flow in from

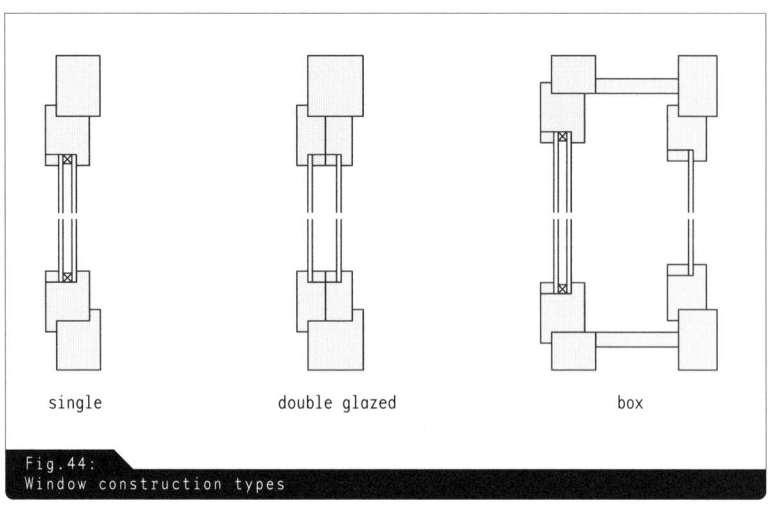

single   double glazed   box

Fig.44:
Window construction types

below, and warm air escapes at the top. As none of the sides is firmly fixed to the frame, the extending mechanism must exert completely even pressure.

CONSTRUCTION TYPES › Fig. 44

Single windows

Single windows are the norm nowadays, as thermopane glazing can provide good heat insulation. So the U_w value of a window with thermopane glazing is about 3.0 W/m²K and with thermal insulation glazing including frame about 1.3 W/m²K.

Double-glazed windows

Before insulating glass was developed, windows were single (U_w value approx. 4.8 W/m²K). Double-glazed windows were much in evidence to improve heat and sound insulation. Two single frames were combined, i.e. opened together as well. If the panes are 40 to 70 mm apart, a slightly better insulation value is achieved in relation to single windows with insulating glass (U_w value approx. 3 W/m²K).

\\Note:
Overall heat transfer coefficient
Window structures have to be evaluated as a complete system in terms of their heat insulation capacity. Windows are allotted a U_w value. The U_w value (formerly k value) states the energetic quality of the entire structural element. The lower the U_w value, the less warmth is lost through the window surface. The U_w value is made up of the individual heat insulation values of the glass (U_g value), the frame (U_f value), and the linear heat transfer coefficients of the glass edge (psi value), taking the area proportions into consideration.

Fig.45:
Box windows (steel)

The sections could be opened up for cleaning. Double-glazed windows are usually supplied as turn, tilt-turn and tilt windows.

Box windows

Old buildings often still have double-glazed windows made up of two simple panes mounted together. These are further apart than the frames in modern double-glazed windows, and are not combined structurally. Now the inner section usually contains insulating glass. The airspace between the panes increases heat and sound insulation. If the two windows placed one behind the other are made into a unit with a continuous lining, usually made of timber, the unit is known as a box window. Both types are usually supplied as turn windows. › Fig. 45

Box windows are often divided by bars, a typical 19th-century window type. The high proportion of frame, the bars, and the offset positioning of the frames mean that a lot of daylight is lost. The box window is a forerunner of today's additional-leaf glass facades. Because they are complex and expensive to manufacture, box windows are mainly used when there are stringent demands on sound insulation or for refurbishment in listed buildings.

Frameless window

In modern windows, it is the frame, not the insulating glass unit, that is the weak point in terms of heat transfer. One possibility for optimizing this lies in reducing the proportion of frame. The chief characteristic of frameless windows is that they have no visible frame or glass retention devices (point holders, clamp profiles) on one side. The glazing consists of stepped-edge glass: the outer pane protrudes over the edge of the inner pane and is glued to the supporting frame. The adhesive can be made out as a continuous black margin behind the outer pane of glass.

Frameless windows can be supplied in most of the opening methods mentioned. However, the glued joint is more delicate and needs more maintenance than a clamp profile.

Fig.46:
Components of a window

FRAMES

Fixed frame

This type of frame is built into the wall structure and the frames of the opening sections are attached to it, or fixed glazing is mounted in it. › Fig. 46

(1a) Frame wood, top section of the fixed frame

(1b) Lower section of the fixed frame (not shown in Fig. 46)

(1c) Side section of the fixed frame

(2) Post (window post), dividing the fixed frame vertically (not shown in Fig. 46)

(3) Rail (crossbar), dividing the fixed frame horizontally

When fitting the fixed frame, there should be adequate tolerance with the wall opening, to avoid tensions and absorb movement in both the structural element and the building. Connections with the building must be slightly elastic or free to slide. › Chapter Fitting structural elements together, Seals

›

Casement frame

The casement frame is the part of the window that is attached to the fixed frame and can be opened. › Fig. 46

(4) Casement frame

(4a) Casement timber, upper section of the casement frame

(4b) Casement timber, lower section of the casement frame (weather bar)

(4c) Casement timber, vertical section of the casement frame

(5) Bar, to divide the casement frame horizontally

(6) Glazing

Windows with two opening sections can be divided by a post, the window post, i.e. a fixed elements that is part of the fixed frame. Alternatively, a rising centerpiece, the astragal, can be used as part of the opening section of the window, in order to cover the joint on this section and the sealing. This is known as a French casement.

French casement

\\ Important:
Permissible tolerances limit deviation from nominal dimensions, from the size, shape, and position of a structural element in the building. The term "tolerance" also includes intended deviations from the theoretical nominal dimensions. This enables compensation for imprecision that is inherent in materials or specific to the manufacturer.

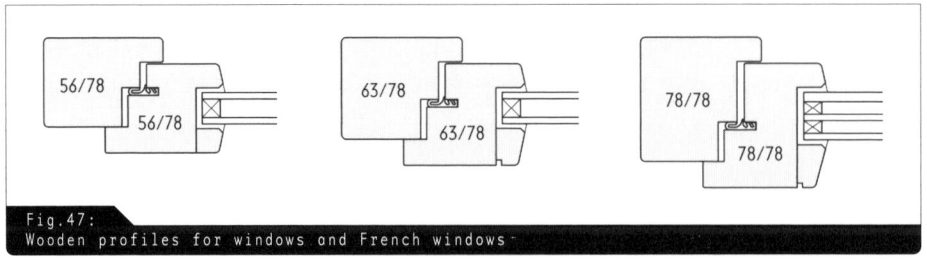

Fig.47:
Wooden profiles for windows and French windows

MATERIALS – SYSTEM WINDOWS
Timber windows

The chief advantages of timber windows are its good heat insulation capacity (comparative thermal conductivity: spruce: $\lambda = 0.11$ W/mK; aluminum alloy: $\lambda = 209$ W/mK), ease of working, and the sustainability of the material. There is no need for elaborate and expensive manufacturing processes or complicated thermal separation of the profile cross sections.

Coniferous timber (pine, spruce, lark, Douglas fir, fir) are mainly used for window construction, and deciduous timber more rarely (oak, robinia). The use of tropical deciduous timber (Meranti, mahogany, Kambala) is declining. The surface of the frame is subject to constant weathering by UV rays, drying, rain, etc. The constant change in the timber's moisture content that this brings about (25–50%) encourages damaging attacks by putrefying fungi, mold or insects. A timber that is suitable for window construction must thus be adequately robust, have a low moisture absorption capacity and show natural resistance. › Fig. 49

Natural timber windows can be additionally protected by surface treatment. Priming is a preventive measure against timber-discoloring fungi, and impregnation prevents moisture-induced rot. A distinction is made between varnishing and covering coats of paint. Please note here: the darker the color, the more the timber will heat up. Beveled or rounded profile edges ensure that the paint will bond with the timber profile more durably.

Structural timber protection is essential when constructing timber windows. Standing water must be avoided, and precipitation water must be able to run off timber profiles and surfaces, i.e. there should no horizontal surfaces.

Profiles   Timber profile cross sections are available in standard sizes and gradations (standard profiles). › Fig. 47 Brief definitions give the profile depth

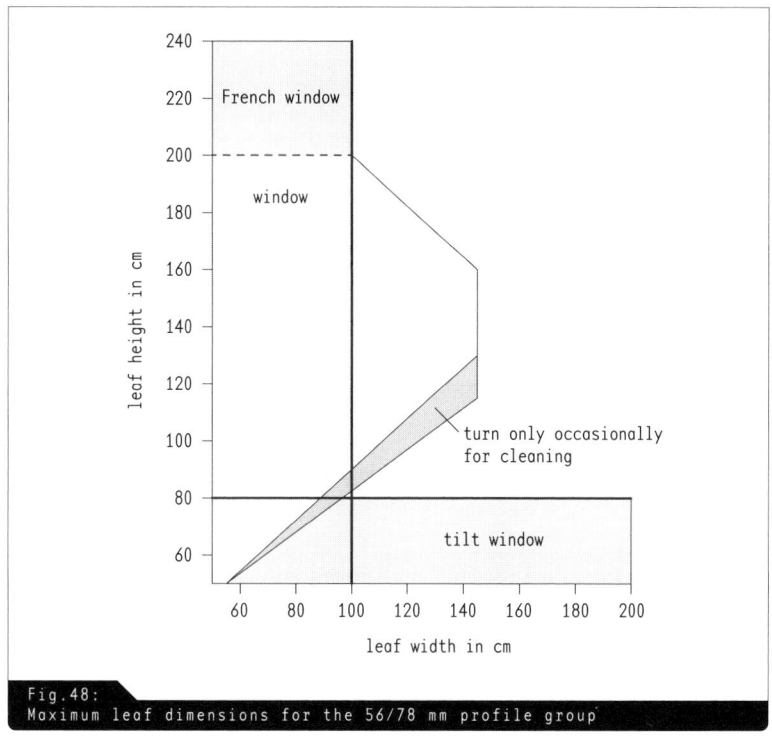

Fig.48:
Maximum leaf dimensions for the 56/78 mm profile group

and profile length in millimeters. U_f values of 1 W/(m²k) can be achieved with window frames in solid wood (e.g. 3-ply glued wooden frames).

Element sizes — The profile size affects the maximum leaf size, both relating to the nature of the opening. The leaf of a tilt window should for example not be higher than 80 cm with a profile cross section of 56/78 mm; the leaf of a French window (turn door) should not be wider than 1 m because of the dead weight and the load on the hinges. › Fig. 48

Metal windows

Metals are very good heat conductors. Steel has 250 times the thermal conductivity of wood, and aluminum has 4 times the thermal conductivity of steel. So metal profiles must be separated thermally in window construction.

There is a wide range of products available for both aluminum and steel windows. The profile dimensions differ considerably. Unlike timber windows, there are no uniform standard profiles fixed.

55

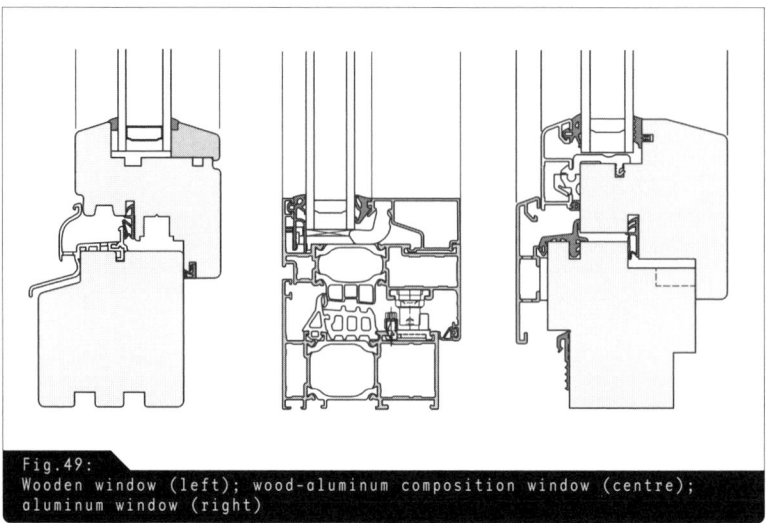

Fig.49:
Wooden window (left); wood-aluminum composition window (centre); aluminum window (right)

Aluminum window

The thermally separated profiles of aluminum windows are made of extruded semi-finished materials. The inner and outer profiles are also separated by plastic pads or rigid foam. Despite the high investment costs (because of the amount of primary energy used in working the raw materials), aluminum windows are economical in comparison with windows of the same size in wood or plastic. Aluminum lasts longer, and is considered particularly easy to maintain and care for. It has low profile tolerances, i.e. the frames are very precisely dimensioned; it is very workable, and very light in weight. › Fig. 49

Points where aluminum windows connect with the rest of the building have to be able to absorb larger temperature-related length changes than timber or steel windows. (Aluminum expands in length by 1.5 mm at a temperature difference of 60 K.) Adequately dimensioned expansion joints between the fixed frame and the building, and inside large window and facade elements must be planned in.

As a rule, the surface is coated, as untreated aluminum oxidizes irregularly and stains. We distinguish between mechanical surface treatments such as smoothing, brushing or polishing, and electronic processes such as anodizing, which produces an even layer of oxide. Aluminum profiles can also be stove-enameled or powder-coated. Powder-coating is achieved by applying the coating material with powder guns and baking it in an oven at object temperatures of about 180 °C.

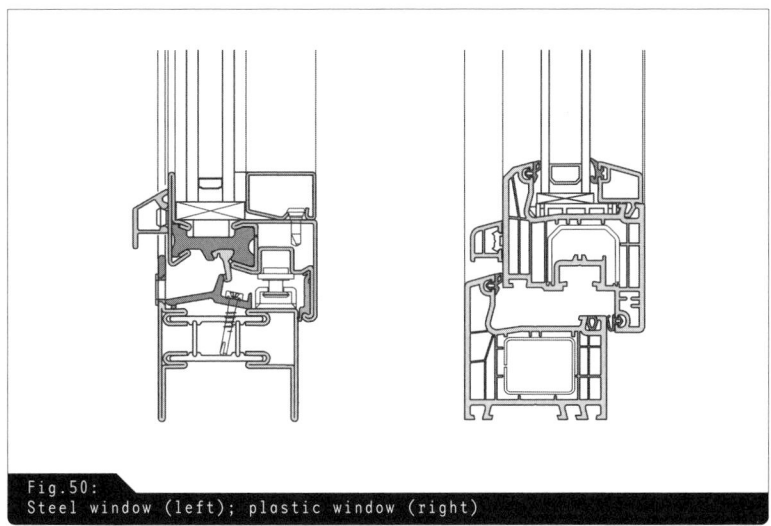

Double-glazed windows (timber-aluminum)

Timber and aluminum double-glazed windows combine the positive properties of both materials effectively. The timber frame with its low thermal conductivity is placed on the inside as the loadbearing structure and the weather-resistant aluminum cladding on the outside as trim and weatherproofing.

Sliding joints should be used to compensate for the thermal expansion differential between wood and aluminum. Condensation must not be allowed to form in the contact zone.

Various construction types can be used for timber-aluminum windows. The external aluminum cladding can be fitted to a standard timber window subsequently. In other systems, the aluminum profiles form the outer glass rebate plane and integrate the rebate seals. Such systems achieve U_f values of 1.3–1.5 W/m^{2}K. Multi-layer timber frames and an efficient insulating central layer (e.g. in polyurethane foam) achieve U_f values of 0.5–0.8 W/m^{2}K.

Steel windows

Steel window frames can be made simply from hot-rolled T or L steel profiles, or as special profiles. Hollow sections are now most commonest, cold-rolled from high-quality strip steel. Steel windows have high bending and torsional rigidity and are more robust than aluminum windows. The frames consist of thermally separated profiles. › Fig. 50

The greatest disadvantage of steel windows is the risk of corrosion, which can be countered with protective paint or galvanization, or by using stainless steel profiles. Steel windows can be stove-enameled or powder-coated.

Plastic windows (PVC, GRP)

PVC profiles Extruded hollow profiles in rigid PVC (polyvinylchloride) are supplied as single or multiple-chamber systems. Multiple-chamber systems have a higher thermal insulation capacity. To make the frame, preprepared extruded profiles are mitered and usually welded. The PVC profile has low thermal conductivity, but is also relatively low in strength, so metal sections are fitted into the chamber profile to provide greater stability. Thermal separation is not required because the metal parts are in the middle of the overall cross section. › Fig. 50

Condensation drainage and the required vapor diffusion compensation to the outside take place via outlet apertures in the front chamber. Most PVC windows are supplied in white. Plastic profiles can also be dyed or coated, but not painted.

For dark colors in particular, warming from solar radiation causes greater longitudinal expansion, because of PVC's high thermal expansion coefficient. The effect of light can also bring about changes in the color shade.

GRP profiles To avoid heat loss via the window frame, i.e. to improve the U_w value of the window, GRP profiles (glass-fiber reinforced plastics) are also used as frame profiles. GRP has low thermal conductivity and is characterized by high strength and rigidity, so no further reinforcement is required. GRP profiles can be combined with aluminum profiles.

GLAZING SYSTEMS

The glazing system is a combination of glass, the glazing rebate and the sealing into the frame. When planning a window construction, the properties required from the glazing system must therefore be considered along with the material and construction of the frame. This applies to the thermal behavior of the glass and the production-dependent pane sizes, and where applicable any special functions for the glazing (heat and sound insulation, fire prevention), the bedding of the glass, and the sealing processes. › Fig. 51

In addition to the thermal transfer coefficient of the window (U_w value), which is expressed in W/m²K, the possible energy gain through the glazing is important for energetic evaluation of a window. Energy gain is defined as energy transmission efficiency or solar heat gain (g value). The g value is calculated from direct solar energy transmission and secondary inward heat transmission (emissions from long-wave radiation and convection). The g value is given for the glazing used in values between 0 and 1 or between 0% and 100%. The higher the value, the more energy is entering the room.

Panes of glass are supplied in a wide range of qualities with specific properties.

Single-layer glass

Float glass

Glass manufacturers Pilkington presented a new production process for flat glass in the late 1950s, the float process. Liquid glass from a furnace runs into a bath of tin at a temperature of 1100 °C. The lighter molten glass spreads out over the molten tin in a ribbon, with two parallel bounding surfaces. Float glass panes are usually between a maximum of 6 and 7 m long, according to production, and between 1.5 and 19 mm thick.

The width is determined by various factors, including the maximum dimensions for transport. If the glass is to be transported on a low loader, the maximum height for passing under bridges of 4 m, the height of overhead traffic light equipment and the turning circle of the vehicles are the restricting parameters. Subtracting the height of the vehicle, this means glass widths of something over 3 m.

\\ Important:
Physical properties of float glass, TSG and HSG:

Specific weight:	2500 kg/m^3
Elasticity module:	70,000–75,000 N/mm^2

Thermal properties:

Thermal conductivity:	0.8–1.0 W/(mK)
U_w value:	< 5.8 W/(m^{2}K)
Transformation temperature:	520–550 °C

Acoustic and optical properties (for thicknesses of 3–19 mm):

Assessed sound reduction index:	22–38 dB
Luminosity transmittance (Lt):	0.72–0.88
Radiation transmittance:	0.48–0.83

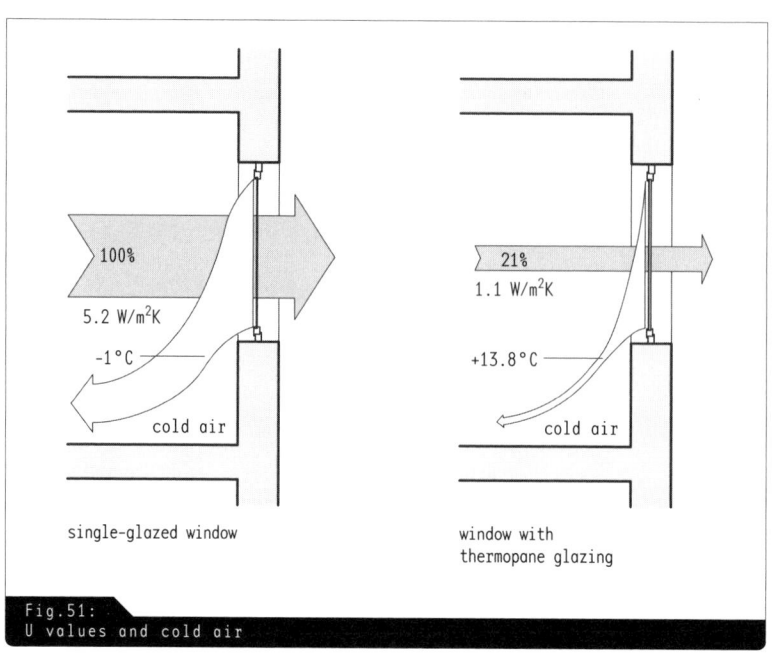

single-glazed window

window with thermopane glazing

Fig.51:
U values and cold air

Tab.2: Examples of U_w values for windows (2004)	U_w value W/m²K
Single-glazed window	4.8
Window with double thermopane glass (details in mm) (4 / 12 air / 4)	3.0
Double thermopane glass (4 / 12 air / 4)	2.7
Triple thermopane glass (4 / 10 air / 4 / 10 air / 4)	2.2
Triple thermopane glass (4 / 8 gas / 4 / 8 gas / 4)	1.7
Double thermopane glass precious metal coated (4 / 20 gas / 4)	1.3
Triple thermopane glass precious metal coated (4 / 10 gas / 4 / 10 gas / 4)	0.9
Double windows/box windows	2.3
Special thermopane glass	0.4
Forced entry resistant glass	1.6

Fig.52:
Glass panels, transparent, translucent

Varying from manufacturer to manufacturer, panes of float glass are manufactured 3.2 m wide and a maximum of 7 m long. Float glass can be colored in the production process. The natural green tinge of float glass can be reduced by a special selection of raw materials, producing "white glass" or "extra-white glass". Surface treatment like rubbing, etching or sandblasting makes the originally transparent float glass translucent. Float glass fragments into large, sharp pieces. It can be processed further to produce a number of products. › Fig. 52

Cast glass

When making cast glass, the liquid glass melt is passed between several pairs of rollers, creating one smooth and one structured or two structured surfaces on the glass. The surface structure makes the glass translucent, the light is scattered. The fracture pattern is the same as for float glass. Figured glass (e.g. U-glass) can be made by the casting process.

Wired glass

The hot glass mass has a wire net, welded at the intersection points and usually in stainless steel, pressed into it by a roller during the manufacturing process. This wire grid holds the parts of the pane together if the glass breaks, and prevents injuries. As a rule, wired glass (local regulations must be consulted here) can be used for overhead glazing. Water penetrating at the edges can lead to corrosion or ice according to the wire inlay, and cause flaking in the glass. Hence the edges of the glass should be sealed or protected by frames.

Thermally treated glass

Tempered safety glass

Heating the pane to the transformation temperature and immediate cooling (e.g. by blowing cold air over the glass) creates additional compressive stress in the glass, which prestresses it.

This change to the structure of the glass raises the flexural breaking resistance of the glass and its thermal shock resistance. If the glass is badly damaged, the result is a tight network of tiny glass crumbs, mainly with blunt edges. Tempered safety glass cannot be processed mechanically after the thermal treatment.

> 💡

Heat strengthened glass

Heat strengthened (partially tempered) glass has a surface tension just large enough so that in case of damage it will break from edge to edge only. Heat strengthened glass (HSG) is not safety glass. It is made similarly to fully tempered glass (TSG), but the air-blowing process is slower, so that the compressive stress building up on the surface is lower than for TSG. Thus, HSG is less likely to break spontaneously than TSG. HSG has considerably greater flexural breaking resistance than float glass and much greater thermal shock resistance.

Multi-layered glass

Laminated glass

Laminated glass consists of at least two panes and an intermediate layer of foil or casting resin. It does not comply with any safety requirements, however.

Laminated safety glass (LSG)

The version that does meet safety requirements consists of at least two panes. So it is described as LSG of float + TSG, or LSG of double HSG, etc. The panes are fixed together by an intermediate layer of casting resin or sheet PVC foil (polyvinyl butyral). The sheets used are elastic and highly resistant to tearing, and they can be colored or calendared. They are inserted between the panes and welded to the glass under heat and pressure. The adhesive properties of PVC sheeting can be impaired if it is permanently wet. Hence the glass, for example as part of an insulated glass fitting, must always be fitted in an air-free rebate clearance to enable glass rebate ventilation. In case of breakage, the glass splinters from the

💡
\\ Important:
Tempered safety glass (TSG) cannot be processed mechanically after thermal treatment, so any drilling or cutting to size must be decided upon and carried out before the tempering.

attached panes with be kept out of the intermediate layer, so that the glass still meets safety requirements in its damaged state.

Additional-leaf glass

Insulating glass units usually consist of at least two panes of glass kept apart by a peripheral joint. The gap between the panes contains dried air or an inert gas to improve thermal or sound insulation. The peripheral connection is essential for impermeability and is usually made using a space, a primary sealant (e.g. butyl), and a secondary sealant (polysulfide). The spacer with its butyl strips is glued to the clean pane, and the second pane is then put in position and sealed with polysulfide.

The spacer has a cavity on the side of the gap between the panes and filled with a desiccating agent. A typical structure for an insulation glass unit is e.g. 6 mm float glass inside, 12 mm gap between the panes, and 6 mm float glass on the outside. > Fig. 53 and Tab. 3

Special glass

For thermopane glass, the thermal insulation properties of the insulating glass are enhanced by adding an inert gas filling to the gap between the panes and/or using three rather than the usual two panes (U_g value 0.5 Wm^2K). The gap between the panes is increased by 10 to 16 cm according to filling.

Inert gases are use to fill the gap between the panes as they are poor heat conductors (krypton produces the best U_g value (0.5 Wm^2K) with a gap of 2×12 mm). At the same time, panes of insulating glass are given a color-neutral coating of a precious metal to reduce thermal conductivity. This is applied to the outside of the inner glass pane.

\\Note:

Manufacturers' standard insulation glass unit sizes

According to manufacturer, the maximum sizes vary between 420 x 260 cm and 720 x 320 cm, with a gross weight of up to 3.5 t. The dimensions of an insulating glass unit are based on the maximum area that can be manufactured. TSG with a thickness of 6–10 mm makes areas of up to 10.9 m² possible. Minimum dimensions for insulating glass units are 24 x 24 cm for float glass combinations, and 20 x 30 cm for TSG combinations. Coating processes are needed according to the properties required (thermal insulation, heat absorption, sound insulation), which can produce different dimensions.

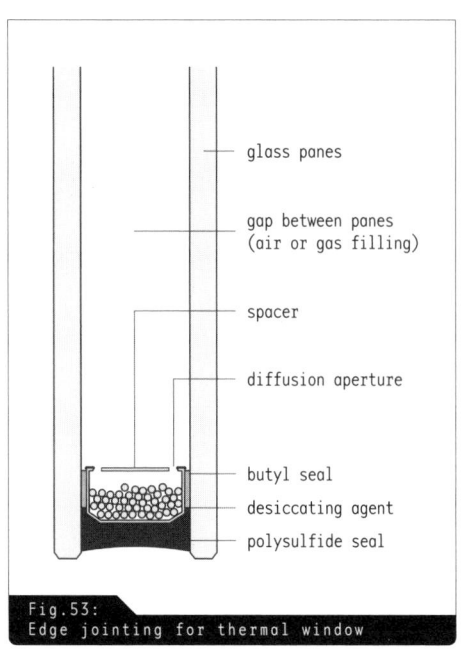

Fig.53:
Edge jointing for thermal window

glass panes

gap between panes
(air or gas filling)

spacer

diffusion aperture

butyl seal
desiccating agent
polysulfide seal

Tab.3:
Building physics specifications for glazing types (as of March 2006)

	U_g value W/m^{2}K	g value %	Lt value %
Single pane glazing (Pilkington Optifloat clear)	5.8	85	90
Double insulation glass with air gap 10–16 mm	3.0	77	80
Double insulation glass 4/16/4 argon, coated (Pilkington Optitherm S3)	1.1	60	80
Solar glass 6/16/6 with vapor coating (flat glass Infrastop Brilliant)	1.1	33	49
Triple insulation glass with 4/12/4/12/4 krypton, coated (Pilkington Optitherm S3)	0.7	50	72
Glass bricks	3.2	60	75
Single profile construction, (flange width) 60 mm (Pilkington Profilit)	5.7	79	86

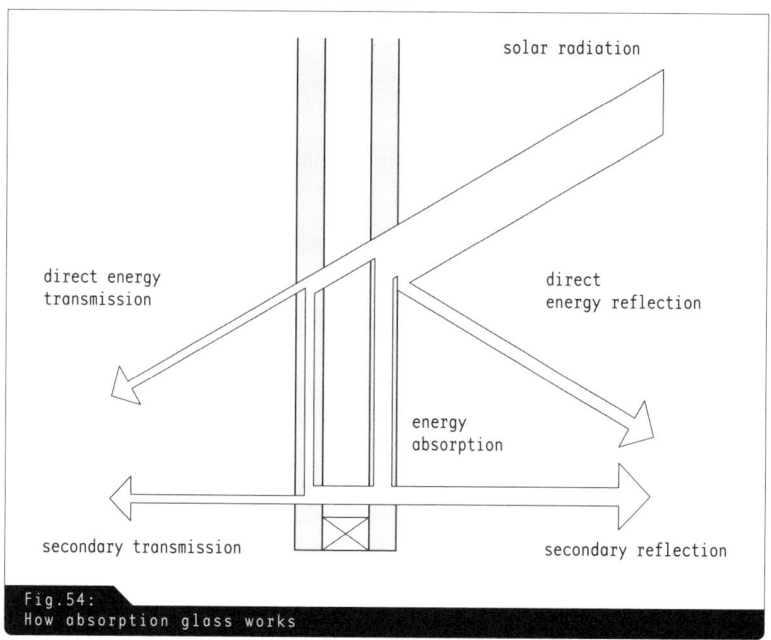

Fig. 54:
How absorption glass works

Heat-absorbing glass

Heat-absorbing glass is intended to prevent rooms from heating up behind glazing, so that additional shading measures can be avoid where possible. This glass is admits a large proportion of light in the visible area of the spectrum, while transmitting little of the heat-generating solar radiation.

We distinguish between two modes of operation, which can also be combined:

- _ Absorption glass is colored by adding metal oxides, so that parts of the incident radiant energy is absorbed and transformed into thermal energy. This is largely dispersed to the outside and in very small quantities inwards, with a delay. › Fig. 54
- _ Reflecting glass works through metallic oxide coating that reflects large amounts of the incident radiant energy (UV and infrared radiation), but largely admits visible light. This usually selective coating is on the inside of the outer pane. › Fig. 55

Switched and variable glazing

More recent developments have addressed glazing that can be switched and varied. This type of glass is identified by its structure, the

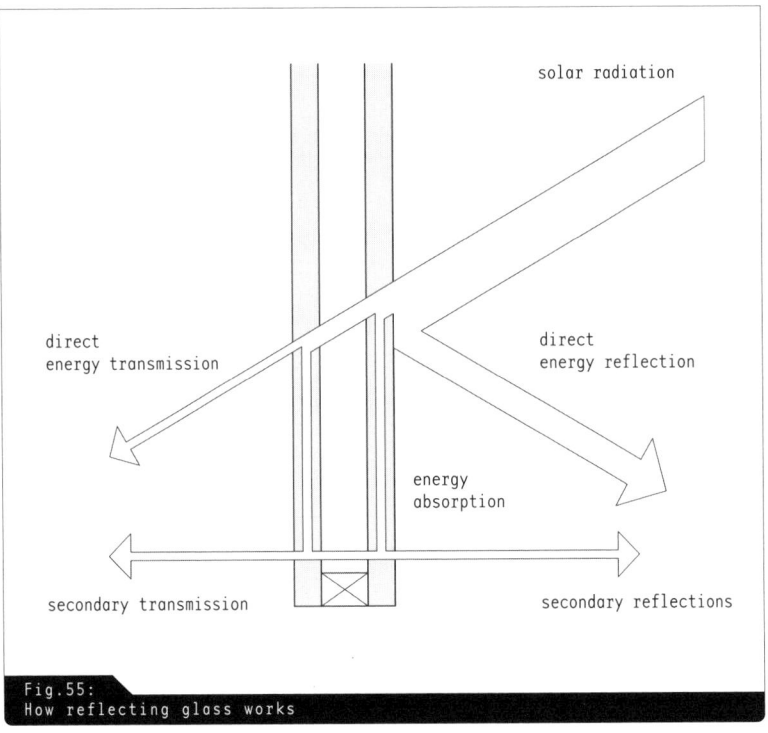

solar radiation

direct
energy transmission

direct
energy reflection

energy
absorption

secondary transmission

secondary reflections

Fig.55:
How reflecting glass works

nature of the switchable layers and the way they are activated (electrochromic, gasochromic, photochromic and thermotropic systems). The degree of transmission can be altered using electric current, gas, thermal or solar radiation in parts of the glazing. In this way, the incident solar energy and the amount of incident light can be reduced or controlled according to the weather, or the time of day or year.

Soundproofing glass The assessed sound reduction index (Rw) provides information about the sound insulation properties of glazing. The sound insulation value of an insulating glass unit can be improved by:

_ Increased pane weight
_ Different pane thicknesses (asymmetrical structure)
_ Using compound panes
_ Greater distance between panes with inert gas filling

The glass used for fire resistance is always considered in the context of the frame and the way it is fastened to the shell. We distinguish between G- and F-category glazing.

G-category glazing prevents flames and combustion gases penetrating for the given time, but does not contain heat from the fire. G-glass can be supplied as special TSG or as laminated glass, in tempered soda-lime glass, for example.

F-category glazing contains flames and combustion gas penetration, and also the spread of heat radiation. This is always required in places where there is a fire escape route behind the fireproofed area. F-category

ρ

\\ Example:
The assessed sound reduction index uses a single value to define the sound reduction properties of a structural component or the sound insulation between room. This value for a structural element depends on frequency. We distinguish between two air sound reduction indices:

R'w: assessed sound reduction index in dB with sound transmission via flanking structural elements
Rw: assessed sound reduction index in dB without sound transmission via flanking structural elements
Characteristic value for air sound reduction
_ Walls, ceilings   R'w
_ Doors, windows   Rw

Q

\\ Important:
Sound insulation value for windows
In Germany sound insulation for windows is divided into sound insulation classes.

Sound insulation class	Window	Assessed sound reduction index
Sound insulation class 1/2	Single window with insulation glass (4 / 12 air / 4)	25–34 dB
Sound insulation class 3	Single window with insulation glass (8 / 12 air / 4)	35–39 dB
Sound insulation class 4	Single window with insulation glass and cast resin filling (9 / 16 resin / 6)	40–44 dB
Sound insulation class 5	Single window with insulation glass and cast resin filling (13 / 16 resin / 6)	45–49 dB
	Double-glazed window, insulation glass (9 / 16 air / 4), single glass (6 mm)	45–49 dB
Sound insulation class 6	Box window: insulation glass (6 / 16 air / 4), single glass (6 mm)	> 50 dB

DIN 4102 fire behavior of building materials and elements – fire retardant glazing

Structural elements	Fire resistance duration (minutes)
Walls, ceilings, beams, columns	F30–F180
Stairs, windows/glazing systems	F30, F60, F90, F120
	G30, G60, G90, G120
Fireproof partitions (doors, gates, flaps)	T30–T180

> 𝒫

glazing has a gel in the gap between the panes. If fire breaks out, the gel foams to create a tough, solid mass.

Fixed glazing can achieve fire resistance classes up to F90. As a rule, an F-glass unit needs general approval in relation to building regulations, which also stipulate the number, type, and position of the attachment points to the shell.

Burglar protec-
tion glass

Burglar-resistant glazing is categorized in resistance classes (0–6), with special categories for bank and post office counters. They can be combined with alarms. Safety glass is burglar- or even bullet-retardant. Burglarproof glass is tested with a mechanically operated axe. Resistance classes are allocated by the number of blows needed to create a square opening with edges of 400 mm.

FASTENING SYSTEMS

Glass mounting

Glazing beads are used to fix panes of glass in frames. They should be fitted on the inside of a window to protect against break-ins, and they should be removable so that the pane can be replaced if the glass is broken. Glazing beads ensure the integrity of glass and seal, absorb horizontal loads (e.g. wind loads) and transmit these into the loadbearing frame cross sections.

The glazing bead must produce even pressure on the glass pane to prevent the glass from breaking. Glazing beads can be screwed or clipped to the frame according to the system used.

Bars

Fixed glazing or opening windows can be divided by bars. These originate in the development history of glass. It used to be possible to produce only small panes, and these were joined together with structural bars to produced large glazed areas. Now that glass is manufactured by the float process, bars are not required, but monument preservation, building regulations or special features of the place concerned can make the use of glazing with bars essential.

Placing glass
– blocking

Panes have to be secured with glazing blocks to disperse the weight of the glass on the frame. Here we distinguish between loadbearing blocks, which support the glass in the frame, and spacer blocks, which secure the spacing between the edge of the glass and the fixed frame. In fixed glazing, the load is dispersed into the fixed frame and its anchorage in the shell. For opening windows, the load is dispersed via the opening frame and the points at which it is suspended (hinges, rollers, etc.). If the window is to function properly, it is essential that the frame and the opening leaf do not jam, twist or otherwise distort. The pane must not touch the frame at any point and the space between the rebate base and the gap between the panes must remain evenly distributed.

Vapor pressure must be equalized between the rebate space and the outside air, and it must be possible to remove condensation water. Vapor pressure equalization apertures must not be subject to direct wind pressure, so covering flaps may be necessary to protect the outlet openings. Vapor pressure equalization with the interior should be avoided, as this can lead to an accumulation of condensed water in the rebate space.

FITTINGS

Fittings are all the mechanical parts of the window that control opening and closing and secure assembly, fixing and use. › Fig. 56 Window and French window fittings combine the opening leaf and the fixed frame. The opening mechanism must be burglarproof, serve as a childproof lock, and ensure that wind and rain do not penetrate.

Fitting systems are supplied as component sets. They can be fitted concealed, (i.e. invisible), semi-concealed, or open, as in decorative fittings, for example. In the case of turn-and-tilt windows, for example, the moving connection of the window leaf with the fixed frame is created by the hinges, mainly drilled hinges, and by additional fittings:

_ Stays: part of the fittings, moved and fixed when opening and closing the window. The leaf is open or shut by pushing along the locking points.
_ Corner pivot rest: the window's rotation point. Supports the weight of the leaf.

Fig.56:
Window fitting

– <u>Scissor</u>: fixed at the top of the fixed frame and attached to the leaf fittings. With the pivot rest, the scissor forms the window's rotation axis, and controls switching from turning to tilting.
– <u>Locking plates</u>: the fittings on the fixed frame attached to the stay locking system. Windows are locked using all these plates, which also secures joint seals even in severe weather conditions.

Each opening type needs its own fittings.

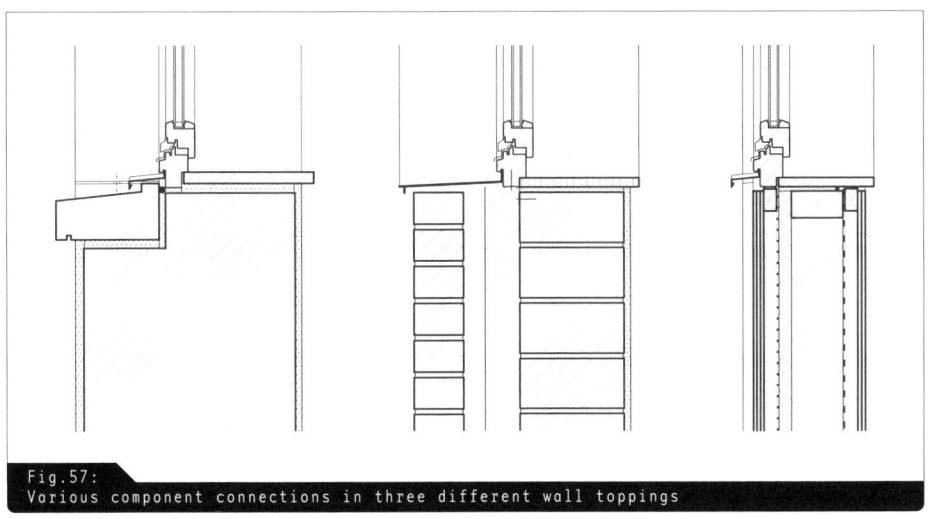

FITTING STRUCTURAL ELEMENTS TOGETHER

BOTTOM OF THE WINDOW

The horizontal conclusion outside a window breast is usually formed by the sill. The following points must be borne in mind to ensure durability and freedom from damage:

- _ The window profile must protrude over the sill and have a drip cap (overlap) to keep it watertight even in driving rain.
- _ The sill must protrude at least 20 mm over the front outer wall edge and also have a drip cap (overlap) to prevent the soiling of the facade below.
- _ The sill must slope slightly outwards (at least 5° or 8%), so that water can run off.
- _ The sill must have an upward lip (e.g. sheet metal or slip-on profile) to prevent the structure from becoming damp. It makes sense to have a lateral overlap of the wall cladding to protect the joint between reveal and sill.
- _ Care should be taken with temperature-related expansion of the sill (length tolerance).

External windowsills

External windowsills can be made of sheet zinc or copper, glass, natural or artificial stone, an upright course of frost-resistant natural or artificial stone, clinker tiles, split tiles, or prefabricated aluminum profiles.

71

Fig.58:
French window finished on the same plane at the bottom

Internal windowsills

Covering for internal window breasts or for radiator niches are usually realized in natural or artificial stone tiles in a bed of mortar or timber or derived timber products (on brackets where appropriate). › Fig. 57

French window

French windows differ from windows with breasts in the form of the lower part of the frame. Where appropriate, the bituminous damp- and waterproofing, terrace of balcony floor covering, and the internal floor fittings must be attached here. In the opening leaf of a French window, the lower horizontal profile is usually higher than for a window, to protect the glazing from splash water. As with a solid door, the bottom of a French window can also be realized on the same plane, by providing a gutter, for example. › Fig. 58

SEALS

Sealing prevents water from penetrating the building through the window structure, and reduces heat loss from uncontrolled air change. We distinguish between seals around the joints between the fixed frame and the shell (compression seals), seals between the fixed frame and the opening leaves (rebate seals), and seals between the frame and the glazing (joint seals).

Compression seals

The seals between the building and the fixed frame balance out tolerances and seal the joints on the outside against wind, driving rain and

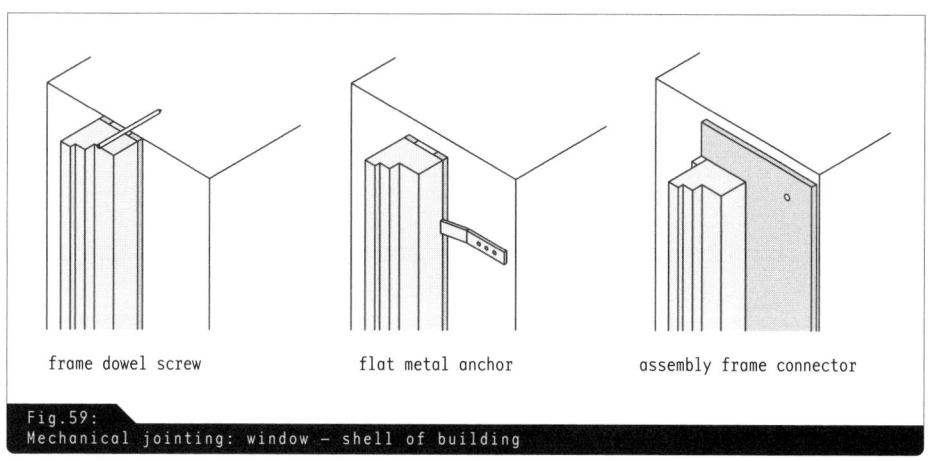

| frame dowel screw | flat metal anchor | assembly frame connector |

Fig.59:
Mechanical jointing: window – shell of building

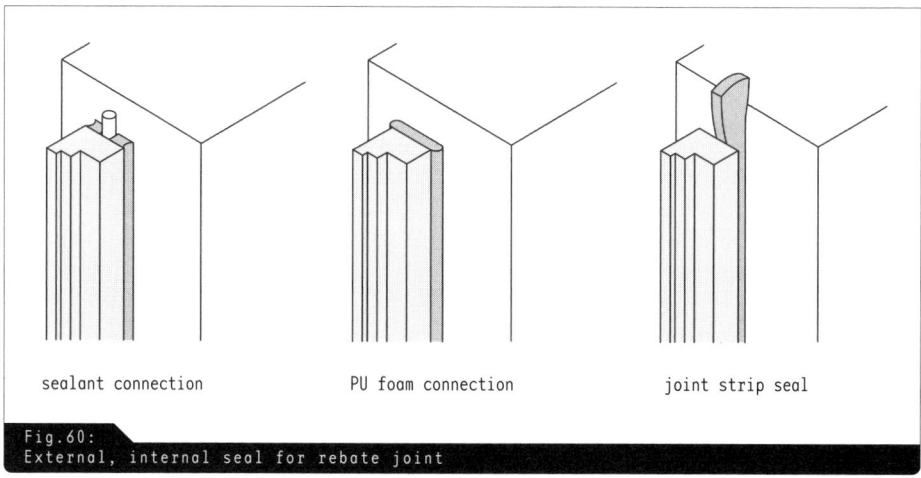

| sealant connection | PU foam connection | joint strip seal |

Fig.60:
External, internal seal for rebate joint

noise, and inside against water vapor diffusion. The window is fixed to the building mechanically in the compression seal area. The fixing elements transfer the vertical and horizontal forces generated. They must allow changes of shape in building and frame without damage. > Figs 59 and 60

Rebate seals   Seals in the leaf rebate between the fixed frame and the opening leaf frame are continuous and ensure adequate sound and heat insulation, and protection from moisture and drafts. Rebate seals consist of seal profiles (e.g. synthetic rubber or neoprene), which are glued into the window leaf

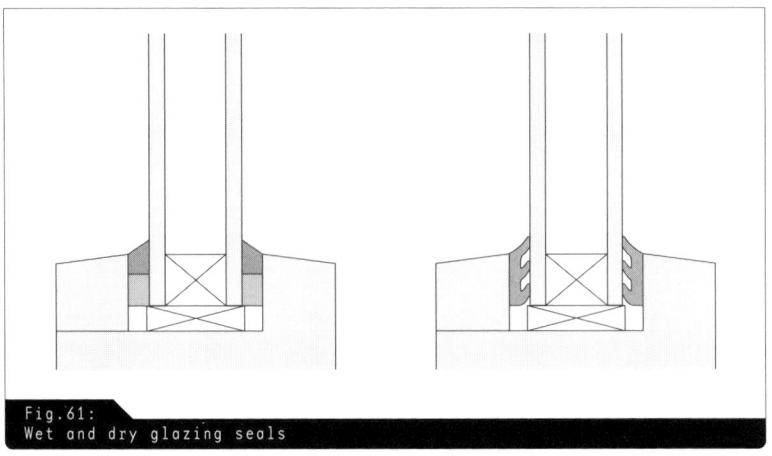

Fig.61:
Wet and dry glazing seals

rebate and where applicable the fixed frame, or pushed into custom-cut grooves. They are used in the form of single or even double and triple seals, and should ideally be replaceable.

Joint seals

Joint seals between frame and glazing unit are supplied for both sides, in continuous linear form. They are manufactured as wet seals in the form of glazing tape (made of sealants such as silicone, acrylate, polysulfide and polyurethane) or with prefabricated seal profiles (e.g. synthetic rubber). > Fig. 61

Prefabricated seal profiles are made by extrusion, so complex profiles can be supplied. Dry seals, unlike wet seals, can be built in with the glazed unit and the glass retention strip in a single process.

\\Note:
Connecting the window frame to the shell:
Connection tolerances between window frame and reveal are absorbed by strip iron as an elastic element, dowel as a sliding connection, or U-shaped frame connectors as an adjustable link. Usually facade or window manufacturers provide a precise specification for the shell apertures, so that adequate tolerance can be allowed when the windows are being planned and made.

\\Example:
Precompressed joint strip (compression strip):
Precompressed, impregnated foam sealing strip on a polyurethane base is supplied compressed to about 15% of the cross section and expands slowly after being fitted into the joint. It fits snugly into the edges of the joint, so that normal material movements at different temperatures are readily accommodated.

JOINTS

Vertical forces are usually dispersed by placing the windows on blocks or wedges that can also be deployed horizontally. Horizontal forces are dispersed by frame plugs, spacer screws, or flat metal anchors, called clamp irons, in the reveal area. The fixing devices must permit uninterrupted sealing by the compression joint.

Joints between fixed frame, masonry rebate and sill, and between sill and breast, are filled with mineral wool or PU foam to form a closed insulation level, but they should also be closed inside and out with weatherstrips. The standard PU foams cannot create durable wind- and vaporproof joints on their own. The best degree of seal – according to the facade cladding – can be achieved by continuously sealing the window frame outside with butyl strips.

Uneven and porous masonry should be rendered to prepare contacts.

\\ Important:
Window solutions:

Chicane
Prevents driving rain and moisture from penetrating. Fitted in the profile: by single or double rebating of frame and fixed frame; in the shell: precipitation is dispersed via the outer or inner rebate by the principle of overlapping several structural elements: reveal/rebate overlap the frame, the frame overlaps the opening leaf frame, the weather bar the sill, and the sill the wall cross section.

Tolerance, building movement
Between frame and shell: adjustable, elastic fixings and continuous joint with mastic joint sealant; between frame and fixed frame: using rebated joints.

Insulation
Positioning on the insulated plane of the wall, use of insulating glass, filling compression joints with mineral wool or PU foam.

Thermal separation
Occurs in profile and glass. In wood through the full cross section, in metal through additional-leaf construction or connection using plastic strips; in plastic using metal chamber profiles; for insulating glass units using spacers and air/gas fillings in the space between the panes.

Sealing
Between frame and glass: with sealing tape and seals of seal profiles; between frame and shell: by rebate, continuous foil sealing or joint sealing strips (see Figs 62 and 63).

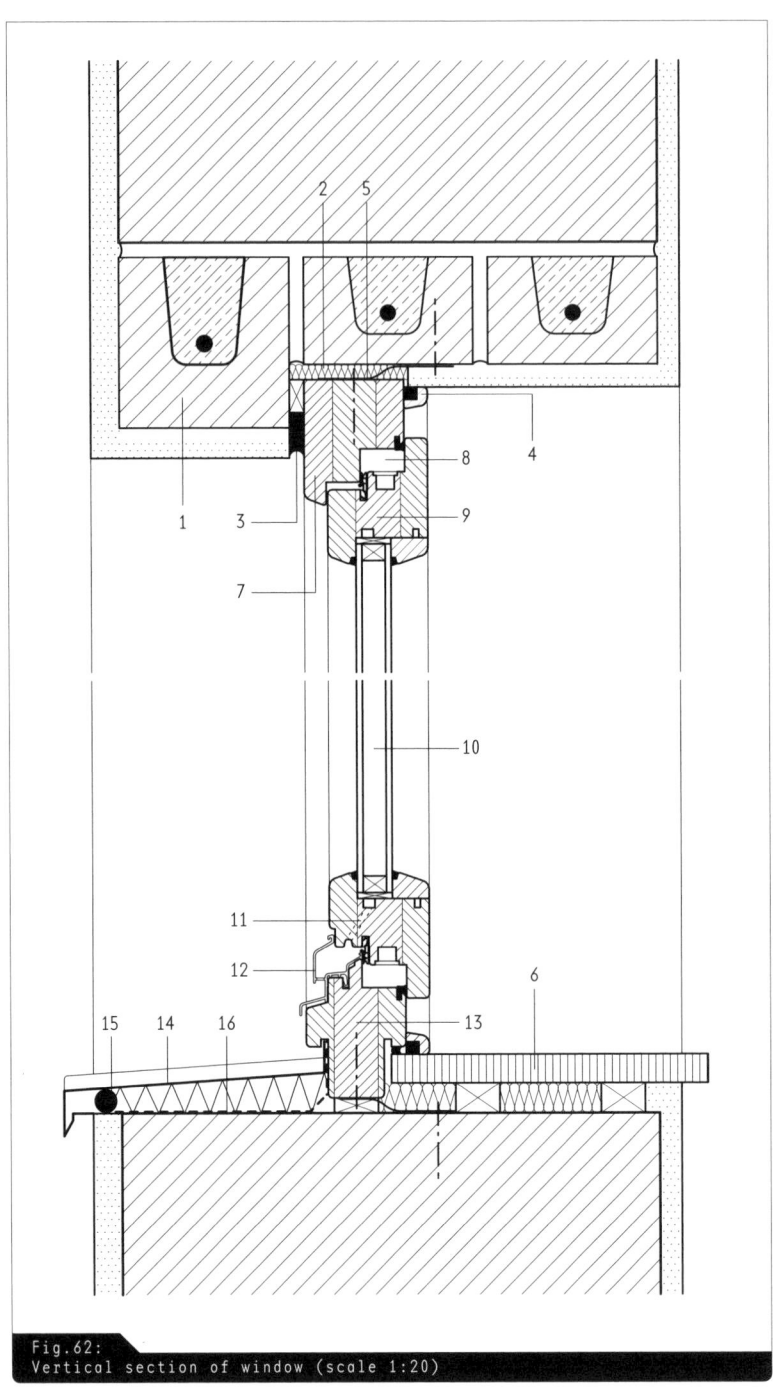

Fig.62:
Vertical section of window (scale 1:20)

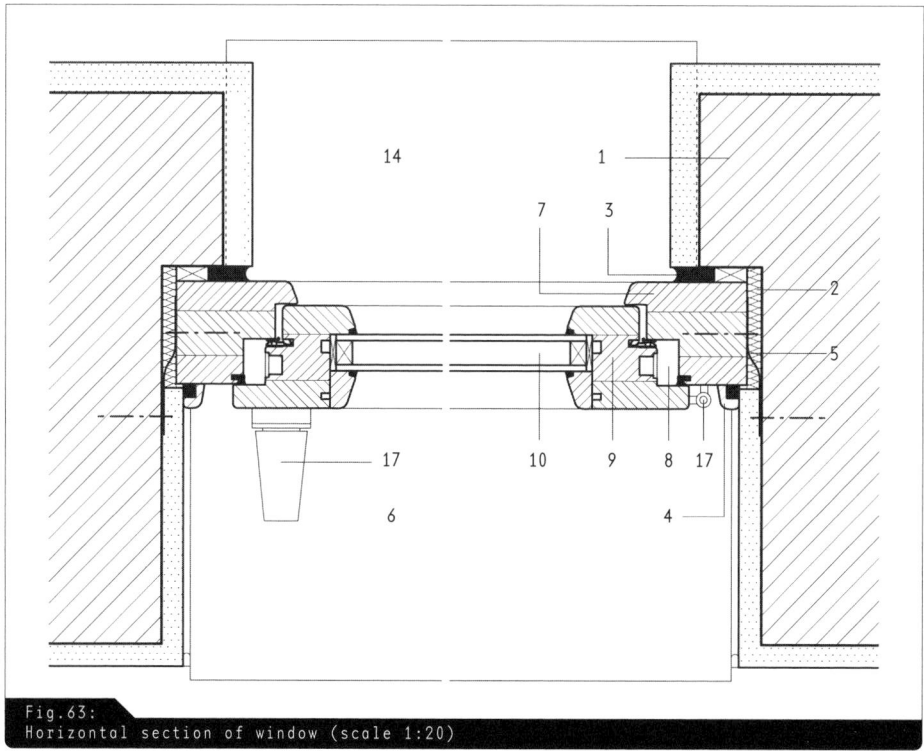

Fig.63:
Horizontal section of window (scale 1:20)

1 Shell connection – internal rebate
  Window lintel: here L-shell
  Window reveal: the external masonry shell
  forms a three-sided rebate (side-top)
2 Rebate insulation
  Mineral wool stuffing or plastic foam (PU foam)
3 Rebate seal
  Internal vapor seal: mastic sealant (e.g. sil-
  icon) on toroid (PU foam); outside: Wind seal
  with sealant tape (compression tape)
4 Covering strip
  Protection and finish for compression joint
5 Covering strip.
  Protection and finish for compression joint
6 Window lining/windowsill, slid on and screwed
7 Fixed frame. Profile: IV 78/78
8 Rebate space
  To accommodate fitting and closing elements
9 Opening leaf frame
  Profile: IV 78/78 with integral rebate and
  frame seals. The opening frame is rebated and
  surrounds the pane of glass on all sides.
10 Insulation glass unit
  8/16 mm, gap between panes 4 mm

11 Vapor pressure compensation
  Ventilation and drainage (condensation) of the
  rebate space via drilled holes
12 Rain protection bar
  Moisture and condensation water can run off
  through openings at the bottom of the bar
13 Bottom fixed frame profile
  Usually has a "drip cap". This overlaps the
  connection to the outer windowsill and protects the joint against precipitation.
14 Weather bar/external sill
  With at least 5° slope: weather bar: aluminum,
  squared off.
15 Lower rebate seal
  Mastic sealant (e.g. silicone) on glazing
  tape secures the windproof edge of the joint
  between the outer artificial stone windowsill
  and the assembly/fixed frame.
16 Windproof connection using windproof film.
  Film all round for windows without rebate.
17 Fitting

IN CONCLUSION

Apertures are a particularly topical architectural subject. Windows are the key to energy-saving planning and resource-friendly building for auxiliary solar heating and for lighting and ventilating rooms naturally.

Refurbishing old buildings is an important area of an architect's work. Here, apertures are important in terms of energetics, their design in particular. The huge building volumes of the post-war decades are hoping for a second chance, and frequently this ends in success or failure simply because of the way the windows are handled. Apertures in listed buildings and ensembles are clearly fewer in quantity, but all the more demanding in terms of the quality challenge they pose.

But design is not limited to successful dimensions and appropriate proportions. A window is a multifunctional structural element that can take up the familiar building repertoire again and also reinterpret it functionally. For example, Bruno Taut was able to add a lucid variant to the concept of the (kitchen) window for his "Onkel-Toms-Hütte" housing estate in Berlin (1926–31), based on his awareness of many models in regional building. Two opening leaves in each case, one an upright rectangle and the other in a somewhat squatter format, are placed above one another, thus creating a single window element in mirror image. This is not just an attractive design, but also enables continuous ventilation through the clearly staggered smaller leaves.

New developments in window mechanics, finish and style are always linked with design-related changes. These are contemporary features that give windows their particular character. The architectural field of apertures as a task for design and construction always requires awareness of structural and design contexts like these, and is of considerable significance when dealing with both old and new buildings.

APPENDIX

LITERATURE

Francis D.K. Ching: *Building Construction illustrated*, 3rd edition, John Wiley & Sons, 2004

Andrea Deplazes: *Constructing Architecture*, Birkhäuser Publishers, Basel 2005

Martin Evans: *Housing, climate and comfort*, Architectural Press, London 1980

Gerhard Hausladen, Petra Liedl, Michael de Saldanha, Christina Sager: *Climate Design*, Birkhäuser Publishers, Basel 2005

Thomas Herzog, Roland Krippner, Werner Lang: *Facade Construction Manual*, Birkhäuser Publishers, Basel 2004

Ernst Neufert, Peter Neufert: *Architects' Data*, 3rd edition, Blackwell Science, UK USA Australia 2004

Christian Schittich, Gerald Staib, Dieter Balkow, Matthias Schuler, Werner Sobek: *Glass Construction Manual*, Birkhäuser Publishers, Basel 2007

Andrew Watts: Modern Constuction: *Facades*, Springer, Vienna, New York 2004

THE AUTHORS

Roland Krippner, Dr.-Ing. Architekt, academic assistant in the Industrial Design Department, TU Munich

Florian Musso, Univ. Prof. Dipl.-Ing., full professor in the Department of Building and Building Material Studies, TU Munich

Academic and editorial assistance: Dipl.-Ing. Sonja Weber and Dipl.-Ing. Thomas Lenzen, Department of Building and Building Material Studies, TU Munich

Series editor: Bert Bielefeld
Conception: Bert Bielefeld, Annette Gref
Layout and Cover design: Muriel Comby
Translation into English: Michael Robinson
English Copy editing: Monica Buckland

Library of Congress Control Number: 2007935228

Bibliographic information published by the
German National Library
The German National Library lists this publica-
tion in the Deutsche Nationalbibliografie; detailed
bibliographic data are available on the Internet at
http://dnb.d-nb.de.

This book is also available in a German
(ISBN 978-3-7643-8465-4) and a French
(ISBN 978-3-7643-8467-8) language edition.

© 2008 Birkhäuser Verlag AG
Basel · Boston · Berlin
P.O. Box 133, CH-4010 Basel, Switzerland
Part of Springer Science+Business Media

Printed on acid-free paper produced from
chlorine-free pulp. TCF ∞
Printed in Germany

ISBN 978-3-7643-8466-1
9 8 7 6 5 4 3 2 1   www.birkhauser.ch

SpringerArchitecture

Horst Sondermann

Photoshop® for Architectural Rendering

2007. Approx. 240 pages. 1000 illus. in color.
Format: 16,5 x 24,2 cm
Hardcover approx. **EUR 44,95**
Recommended retail price. Net price subject to local VAT.
ISBN 978-3-211-71591-8
Due September 2007

Photoshop is the worldwide market leader among image editing software. Along with its classical use for photography and web design, it is also an important 3D-modeling tool. It is used to generate textures and for the post-production of rendered stills. In architectural terms, it can be said that Photoshop is used in all workflow phases, whether to generate and process planning layouts, to produce material textures for virtual modeling or for the final assembly of photographed and rendered image components.

This volume features solutions for typical everyday tasks and helps planners, architects and students achieve satisfying results with the help of Photoshop software.

SpringerWienNewYork

P.O. Box 89, Sachsenplatz 4–6, 1201 Vienna, Austria, Fax +43.1.330 24 26, books@springer.at, **springer.at**
Haberstraße 7, 69126 Heidelberg, Germany, Fax: +49.6221.345-4229, SDC-bookorder@springer.com, springer.com
P.O. Box 2485, Secaucus, NJ 07096-2485, USA, Fax +1.201.348-4505, service@springer-ny.com, springer.com
Prices are subject to change without notice. All errors and omissions excepted.